D1532719

Fueling

the Future

FUELING THE FUTURE

Janet Pack

Educational Consultant
Helen J. Challand, Ph.D.
Professor of Science Education, National-Louis University

Technical Consultant
Michael Brower
Director of Research, Union of Concerned Scientists

CHILDRENS PRESS®
CHICAGO

A production of B&B Publishing, Inc.

Project Editor: Jean Blashfield Black
Editor: Terri Willis
Designer: Elizabeth B. Graf
Cover Design: Margrit Fiddle

Artist: Valerie A. Valusek
Computer Makeup: Dave Conant
Photo Researchers: Marjorie Benson
                      Kathy Brooks Parker

Printed on Evergreen Gloss
50% recycled preconsumer waste
Binder's board made from 100% recycled material

Library of Congress Cataloging-in-Publication Data

Pack, Janet
    Fueling the future / Janet Pack
        p. cm. -- (Saving planet earth)
    Includes index.
    ISBN 0-516-05512-7
    Summary: 1. Explains how fossil fuels pollute the environment and
discusses safer alternatives both presently and potentially available.
2. Fossil fuels--Environmental aspects--Juvenile literature. 3. Coal-fired power
plants--Environmental aspects--Juvenile literature. 4. Automobiles--Motors--
Exhaust gas--Environmental aspects--Juvenile literature. 5. Renewable energy
sources--Juvenile literature. [1. Fossil fuels--Environmental aspects. 2. Energy
development.]
I. Title. II. series.
TD196.F67P33 1992
333.79--dc20
                                      91-34602
                                          CIP
                                          AC

Cover photo—© Imtek Imagineering/Masterfile

Copyright © 1992 by Childrens Press®, Inc.
All rights reserved. Published simultaneously in Canada.
Printed in the United States of America.
1 2 3 4 5 6 7 8 9 10 R 00 99 98 97 96 95 94 93 92

TABLE OF CONTENTS

Chapter 1

Gray Skies, Brown Water

DIRTY SMOKESTACKS DOMINATE what was once a lovely valley. The furnaces of the old machinery factory churn out heavy, black smoke, as they have for years. The dirty residue settles onto the nearby town. The houses are coated with grit, and soot settles in the gutters. Sometimes it is nearly impossible to see the sun through the gray haze. The air smells terrible.

But the dirt and the odor are the least of the problems. The smoke has other, more lasting, effects as well. Nearby streams and lakes can hardly support any life at all. The trees in the area are turning brown—they are dying. Few birds swoop through the sky. Most of them are already dead, or they've flown away.

And the problems get even worse. Many of the people in the town cough a lot and complain about the taste of their drinking water. They frequently see doctors about their health problems. Often their ailments are the symptoms of such serious diseases as cancer, asthma, and emphysema—a deadly lung condition that makes it more and more difficult to breathe. Their children get sick often, and the older people don't live very long.

Sound scary? It is. Many European regions, such as eastern Germany, Hungary, Yugoslavia, and Poland, are facing these frightening and widespread problems—all because their factories are out of date and continue to belch out poisonous smoke. There is no money to build new, more efficient factories. People in these areas work in the old factories because they have no other way to make a living. All they can do is try to make the best of their dangerously polluted lives.

Trouble from Fuels

What is the reason for the lethal black smoke? What causes the bad-tasting water, the smog, the dying trees? Fuels are to blame—specifically fossil fuels.

Fossil fuels are compounds that formed within the Earth's crust in ancient times. We remove them and burn them to create energy. They are called "fossil," because they are the remains of living organisms—mostly plants—from prehistoric times.

Coal, natural gas, and oil, also known as petroleum, are the three kinds of fossil fuels. People around the world depend on these substances to power homes, businesses, industries, and transportation.

The harmful effects of burning fossil fuels go beyond eastern Europe, which is second only to the United States in its use of oil and coal. China, India, the Soviet republics, Japan, Central and South America, Canada, and the United States are all experiencing the same difficulties in varying degrees. Africa and other developing areas are having increasing problems.

When fossil fuels are burned, they release harmful chemicals that can pollute lakes, endangering all living things in them. This lake in Ontario, Canada, has been acidified by pollution.

These problems are not new. In 1930 in Belgium's Meuse Valley, poisonous smoke from factories blanketed towns. With no wind to blow it away, many people in that valley died in the choking fumes. Donora, Pennsylvania, had a similar environmental episode in 1948. More people died.

London, England, which is naturally foggy, was once known for its terrible problem with smog, a combination of smoke and fog that hangs in the air. The situation is now much improved, but in 1952 a particularly heavy smog caused severe asthma attacks, car accidents due to poor visibility, and many deaths.

Serious problems arise more slowly, too.

Though some of our pollution problems are clearing up, much of our air and our water gets dirtier every day. Since 1920, energy demands have doubled every twenty years. This means that today we're using more than six times as much power and fuel as people did then! Nations, states, and cities have been so busy building thriving industries that they have not kept our planet clean and thriving.

The emissions from this smokestack at a Nevada generating station are the products of coal being burned to produce electricity.

The element carbon is part of all living things. When fossil fuels are burned, most of the carbon is released into the atmosphere. Industries that burn fossil fuels send 3 *billion* tons (2.7 billion metric tons) of carbon into the atmosphere every year.

FACT

Soot, Ash, and Smoke

With adult supervision, hold a Pyrex pie plate or piece of glass over a burning candle flame. Use tongs or an oven mitt. Notice the black soot forming on the glass. This is carbon. Not all of the wax burned efficiently and completely, so some carbon was deposited on the glass. Most of the rest of the carbon atoms mixed with oxygen atoms in the air and produced an invisible gas called carbon dioxide (CO_2), which is important to living things.

The soot on the plate shows what happens when fossil fuels burn. The incomplete burning of fossil fuels produces soot and ash, which often appear in the air as smoke.

The next time you grill hamburgers over charcoal in your backyard, look at the briquettes burning. Notice the amount of smoke they give off. When the fire goes out, notice the fine particles left behind. This ash is part of the charcoal that was not burned. When the fire was burning, these tiny particles floated upward with hot air and made smoke.

If you live in a big city, or if you visit one soon, take a look at the sky. Is it hazy and brown? Does it have a bad odor? The air is probably filled with smog. In smog-covered cities, the air is loaded with ash, soot, and other pollutants—the results of burning fossil fuels.

Air Quality. Nature has its own method of using up some of the chemicals in the air. In a process called *photosynthesis*, plants absorb CO_2 from the air and water from the soil, and use them to make sugar, which gives the plants energy to function and grow. It's estimated that plants remove nearly

100 billion tons (90 billion metric tons) of carbon from the atmosphere each year.

Recent inventions used by industries and automobiles have helped clean the air, too, by reducing the amount of harmful chemicals released into the atmosphere. But it may be too late. The pollution produced in previous years is still in our environment. There are few places around the world where the air remains as clean and pure as it was 100 years ago.

Air pollution contributes to water pollution, too, because particles from the air often settle out into bodies of water. Today, it's rare to find a source of water that is unpolluted.

These are dangerous situations.

Through photosynthesis, plants such as Douglas firs (above) *are able to remove a good deal of the carbon that enters the atmosphere from car exhaust* (below).

Without clean air and water, nothing on this planet can live. And yet we need fuel, too. Most of these pollution problems are caused by our burning of fossil fuels, which provide 88 percent of the power demanded by the nearly 5.5 billion people who live and work in the world.

FACT

Fossil fuels are created by very slow processes. Plant and animal remains must collect and be compacted, decay, and be heated under very specific conditions to form fuels. But today, we are using up fossil fuels very quickly. In only one year, people use the amount of energy that it took the Earth about a million years to produce in the form of fossil fuels.

Pollution

All fossil fuels create pollution when they are burned, especially coal and petroleum products, which do not burn as cleanly as natural gas. They send particles and gases into the air. Because they are used by millions of people every

Modern coal miners dig for coal in shafts far underground, using heavy machinery to get at deposits that were once nearly impossible to reach.

One of the reasons fossil fuels are popular is that they are comparatively easy to obtain. This oil-drilling platform is located off the coast of Greece.

day, fossil fuels are the largest contributors to air and water pollution.

If fossil fuels cause so many problems, why do we use them? Why not just find something else?

We use them because oil, coal, and natural gas are readily available. They are fairly easy and inexpensive to obtain from mines and wells. This makes fueling huge industries, such as steel mills and car assembly plants, cheap. It also makes the cost of heating buildings very reasonable. Inexpensive energy is in great demand all over the world.

So this is the situation we are in today—on a path that seems almost certain to damage our habitat and make life more difficult for all living things. But we can keep that from happening if we map out a new course!

Before we begin to chart a safer course for fueling the future, though, we must understand how we got into this situation in the first place. We need to learn how we can use less fossil fuel. Better yet, we must examine other energy sources that will be kinder to our Earth.

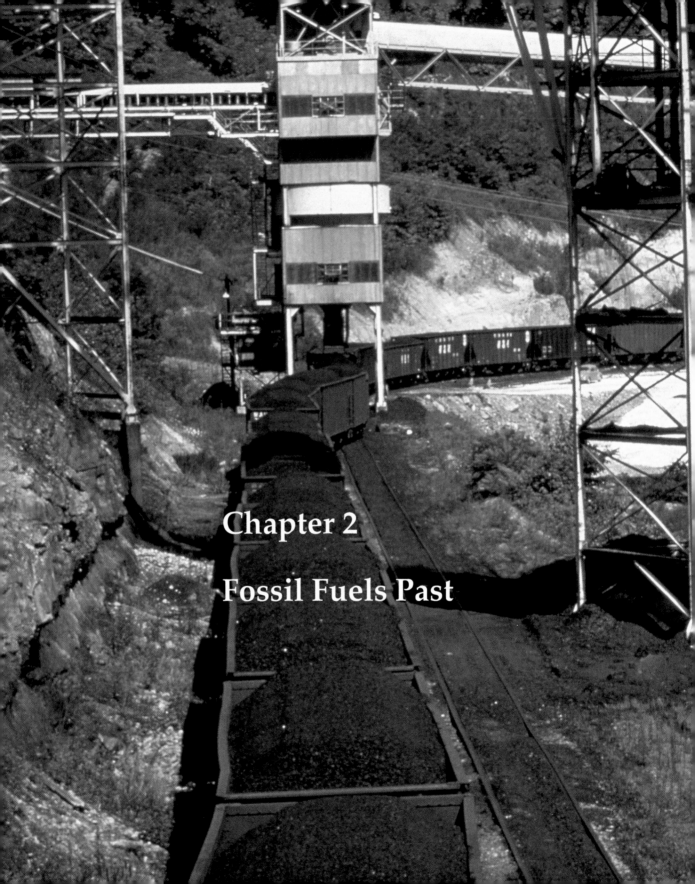

Chapter 2

Fossil Fuels Past

THE SERIOUS POLLUTION PROBLEMS we face as a result of burning fossil fuels are relatively modern, when you consider how long people have been using fossil fuels.

Archeologists suggest that ancient hunters might have chased animals into sticky petroleum tar pits where they were easily killed. Natural gas seeps—areas where gas comes to the Earth's surface through cracks in rocks—were known in Persia (now Iran), between 6000 and 2000 B.C. Some people there worshiped "eternal fires," which were probably seeps that had been ignited by lightning. Early tribes considered fossil fuels gifts from their gods.

Wales has coal mines that were worked during the Bronze Age, about 3000 B.C. These are some of the oldest mines in Europe. The Chinese used coal for heating and cooking as early as 1100 B.C. More than 2,500 years ago they discovered deposits of natural gas. They piped it through hollow bamboo stalks to fuel fires for cooking and for evaporating seawater for salt. They used petroleum to make ink.

Some native tribes in what is now the United States used *burning stones*—their name for coal—instead of wood for fires. Other people discovered that tar and oil were good for weatherproofing houses and making torches. Weapons such as flaming arrows were important in wars. They were made by coating arrows with tar and setting them on fire.

Where the Fuels Came From

Though these uses for fossil fuels are many centuries old, the fossil fuels themselves are even older. They began to form at about the time the first grasses and trees appeared on the Earth—long before the time of the dinosaurs.

Searching for deposits of coal underground, a geologist (above) *examines cores of soil carved out of the Earth by a drilling rig. A large bucket* (right) *is used to scoop coal from a surface mine.*

Coal. Coal is created mostly from decaying vegetable matter, such as primitive swamp plants, that fell into a marsh or bog. Over millions of years, soil, rock, and volcanic ash piled on top, becoming heavier and heavier. This compressed the decaying matter, squeezing out water and making it very hot.

Scientists still don't fully understand the lengthy chemical processes that turned the mass of vegetable matter into coal. They do know that it first changed into *hydrocarbons*, which are chemical compounds made of carbon and hydrogen. Eventually, the hydrocarbons became coal, which is almost pure carbon.

There are many different kinds of coal, ranging from brownish-red *lignite* to harder, darker *bituminous*, and *anthracite*, which is black, shiny, and very hard.

People get at coal by pit mining and strip mining. In pit mining, tunnels are dug deep into the Earth so that the coal can be carved out. In strip mining, long layers of soil, only a few feet deep, are peeled away from the surface.

Oil. Oil was formed in much the same way as coal. Where liquid hydrocarbons remained within the hot, buried mass of vegetation, it stayed in fluid form instead of hardening. Oil appears as a thick, blackish liquid, a brown, light-textured liquid, or a black, sticky tar.

Most of it is found underground, usually along with natural gas. It can also be found in a rock called shale or in sand. And natural leaks called petroleum seeps are found in many parts of the world.

Today, people drill wells to bring oil to the Earth's surface both on land and in the sea. The oil is then run into storage tanks or ships through pipes. Later it is transferred to a refinery where it is chemically changed or separated into needed products, such as gasoline.

Natural Gas. Natural gas is mostly methane (CH_4)—a gas produced by rotting vegetation—mixed with lesser amounts of other gases. Methane is a colorless, odorless gas that burns almost completely, releasing very little soot or smoke into the atmosphere.

While oil often needs to be processed in some way before it can be used for fuel, natural gas can be used exactly as it comes from the ground.

A common method for pumping oil is through the use of "nodding donkeys," which pull the fuel up from its underground deposits. These machines are common sights in areas where oil is found.

17

When it was first discovered, natural gas was thought to be a waste product, and it was not collected. Today, workers drill to locate natural gas deposits, since it is an important energy source.

The Growing Use of Fuels

Until the middle of the 1600s, wood or charcoal was used for heating houses and cooking. Charcoal is made from wood that has been partially burned without oxygen, so that gases in it are driven off. It burns hotter and more cleanly than wood. Wood and charcoal also powered most of the few small industries that existed then.

People living in parts of Ireland and Africa, or other areas where wood was scarce, often used animal droppings or peat for fuel. Peat is made up of compacted and partially decayed plants, kind of like unfinished coal.

In those days, people did not cook by setting the thermostat on an oven to a certain temperature. Instead, they learned by experience how much fuel it took to bake bread or to roast meat. Ovens were usually outside, away from the house, in case of fire. Some ovens were used by entire villages. Kettles set over fires on hearths or hung from spits were commonly used in houses.

Petroleum, natural gas, and coal are found only in certain areas of the world. Geographically, the most concentrated fuel is coal. Ninety-five percent of all coal deposits are found in the Northern Hemisphere. Most developing countries, which need coal, are in the Southern Hemisphere.

FACT

Blacksmiths relied on years of training. They knew the temperature of a fire by the color of its flames. They were able to bring fire to the proper temperature for working copper, brass, bronze, iron, tin, and even steel.

Light was provided by oil lamps and candles. Most lamp fuel came from pressed olives and other vegetable oils, or from whale blubber. Candles were usually made from animal fat, called tallow. The flickering light from candles was poor compared to the light from the electric bulbs we know today. Several candles or oil lamps were needed to light a single room.

A boy from El Salvador collecting wood for his family to use in cooking. Such fuel is still the basic energy source for much of the world.

Now and Then

About one-fifth of all energy consumed in the United States is used in homes. Most of this energy comes from fossil fuels. Are we using more energy today than our grandparents did?

List all the appliances and devices in your home that use some form of energy. Go all over the house, from basement to garage. Look for lamps, refrigerator, stove, hot curlers, vacuum cleaner, washer, lawn mower, etc. One household had 137 such items. How many do you have?

Now sit down with your grandparents or other senior citizens. Find out what appliances they had when they were young.

They may have had a windmill to pump water, a wood-burning stove, perhaps an icebox and a push mower. There were few electrical tools in the workshop. Though the use of coal and oil was fairly common then, much of the energy they used was renewable—wind, water, wood, muscles.

But just because we have more appliances today doesn't mean we have to use as much energy as we do.

Work out a plan with your family to conserve electricity, gasoline, heating oil, and natural gas. Turn off lights when you leave a room. Bake only on cool days. Limit car rides. What are some other things you can do?

We need to save what fossil fuels we have—the world has a limited amount of them. It takes about a million years for the Earth to make the fossil fuels people use in one year. There seems to be plenty of coal, petroleum, and natural gas for the next several decades. But it's very difficult to reach the available supplies without damage to the environment.

New Fuels are Found

During the early 1700s in Europe and Great Britain, industries requiring fuel began to increase. Populations were growing, and additional land was cleared for agriculture. People realized that their huge and beautiful forests, which provided the wood needed for fuel, were shrinking. It was time to find new, easily obtainable, and more efficient fuels.

Wells and Mines. By about 1628, oil wells had already been established in Europe. Italy and Romania were two of the first countries where small drilling companies sank wells. The owners wanted petroleum that could be refined into kerosene to burn in lamps.

As oil is heated, different parts of it turn to vapors at different temperatures. The vapors are then cooled, so that they again became liquid. One of those vapors is kerosene— a nearly pure fuel that burns with less smoke than unrefined oil. This refinement process was probably invented by Arabs who invaded Spain in the 1300s.

Unfortunately, more wells came up dry than produced oil. No one knew then how petroleum collects underground,

One of the first ways people learned about oil and its uses was through oil seeps, where the fuel comes to the surface naturally.

so they could only guess where to drill the wells. Drilling for oil was a risky, expensive business.

As demand rose for new fuels, people in Great Britain, Poland, China, and elsewhere looked for coal deposits. They dug large pit mines into the Earth and began selling coal to factories and individuals. Coal was much easier to get than oil. And coal was also an excellent replacement for wood.

Industry and Coal

People began to use coal more and more to power machines and make their work easier. Industries grew throughout Europe.

Since coal was a cheap fuel that burned easily, it helped industrial growth in the 1700s. No one then worried about the harmful emissions it sent into the atmosphere when it was burned.

Abraham Darby, owner of a small copper and brass foundry in Shropshire, England, decided to use coke as a fuel. Coke is coal that has had the impurities burned from it. It burns more evenly than regular coal. Since there was a lot of coal in the area, coke was inexpensive and easy to make. Darby's business gained a reputation for high-quality metal goods.

In 1707 John Thomas, Darby's employee, discovered a way to make even purer coke. This meant that almost any type of coal could be used in furnaces after it had been processed into coke. This knowledge quickly spread.

Coal's reputation as a good, cheap fuel was made. It fired the Industrial Revolution that started in Great Britain in the early 1700s. The coke could be burned to boil water, which made steam to turn machines.

Factories with huge smokestacks were built in Great Britain, then in Europe, and then in North America and much of the rest of the world. They changed the landscape. Coal-fired steam engines blackened the skies with smoke. The smoke began to fill the air with harmful particles. Villages became dirtier as soot settled onto the buildings.

After only about two or three decades of rapid industrial growth, London became known for its "pea-soup" fog, which sometimes settled over the city for days. The fog was actually smog from the coal fires that heated homes and fueled industries. The smog, filled with particles that hurt human lungs, made people cough and irritated their eyes. People who had asthma or other lung ailments such as tuberculosis suffered greatly. Many died.

Pit-Mine Perils. Even though the use of coal was fouling the air, industry leaders continued to demand more and more coal for their factories. Pit mines were dug larger and deeper. In the early 1700s, most mines went no more than 300 feet (90 meters) below the surface. But then miners began to tunnel sideways as well as downward. The deeper the mine, the more danger to the miners. Timber supports were used to help stabilize tunnel walls and ceilings.

Flooding was another constant threat in mines. A leak could spring through a wall weakened by pressure from an underground lake or stream. The miners had to patch leaks quickly, to keep the mine from filling with water. Pumps were used to keep tunnels fairly dry.

Underground gases, particularly methane, became more dangerous as the miners dug deeper. Most natural gas has little or no odor. Without realizing it, miners sometimes

Coal mining is a dangerous occupation. Mine shafts can flood or collapse, killing miners. And all the coal dust that miners breathe in while working can lead to a serious illness called black lung disease.

walked into a pocket of gas and became unconscious within minutes. Sparks struck from a hard rock wall by tools or a machine close to methane could cause a deadly explosion. Miners used to carry caged canaries into their work areas. If the birds' behavior was unusual or if they died, the miners knew gas was present and fled.

Miners have long faced another danger, too, one which is still present. A sickness called black lung disease haunts the industry. It is caused by breathing in coal dust for an extended period. Soot builds up in the miners' lungs, and eventually causes their lungs to stop working properly. The men often die gasping painfully.

Oil and Gas

Coal was still widely used in the mid-1800s, but businessmen began to look to other fuels for their machines. They turned to oil as a major source of power.

From about 1860 onward, oil-drilling rigs seemed to spring up overnight in fields, on the outskirts of towns and cities, and even in backyards. Many "wildcatters," the people who dug oil wells, struck natural gas before oil began to flow from the wells. At first, the natural gas was considered a waste product, and most of it was burned. Eventually, when they realized the uses for natural gas, the oilmen began to collect it, and then to actively search for it.

The first successful natural gas well in the United States was dug by William Hart in Fredonia, New York. He started the Fredonia Gas Light Company with a single well that was

27 feet (8.2 meters) deep. Modern wells are up to 30,000 feet (9,144 meters) deep.

New companies sprang up to lay pipes that delivered gas into cities and towns for businesses. Soon homeowners wanted gas lines laid to their houses for lighting and cooking, because the gas burned cleanly and didn't smell. So more pipes were run along streets and into houses. Gas replaced kerosene and other smelly, smoky, petroleum-based oil lamps in many areas.

Oddly enough, much of the gasoline used during this period was made from coal. Very few people like Mr. Hart realized the value of the natural gas vented from wells. After mining, bituminous coal is coked (heated) usually without air. This separates hydrogen, methane, and carbon monoxide. This combination of gases, called coal gas, is then recovered and used just like natural gas.

Busy oil fields, such as the Burkbenett Oil Field in Texas shown here, were quickly developed wherever oil was found in the late 1800s and early 1900s.

FACT

Natural gas has very little odor. Gas companies decided many years ago to add a mixture of chemicals that give it a distinctive rotten-egg smell. The scent alerts people to gas leaks, which can cause fires and asphyxiation if not detected.

Fueling the Automobile

Between 1908 and 1913 a new invention began to change life-styles around the world. The automobile arrived on the scene, making transportation quicker and easier than ever before. Henry Ford not only designed the popular Model T automobile, but he also mechanized its construction. He developed an assembly line that made the car cheap enough for lots of people to buy.

Within a few years, Fords were available to anyone with $500. No longer toys for the wealthy, the "horseless carriages" changed the attitudes of Americans toward travel. Cross-country trips, difficult and uncomfortable in horse-drawn vehicles or on trains, became possible for every family with a car as roads were paved. Trucks soon replaced horses for hauling cargo.

The vehicles that began to fill up the roads were powered by gasoline. A typical gasoline engine has several round tubes called cylinders. Inside the cylinders are rods called pistons, and two valves. One valve lets in fuel and air, the other valve lets out the exhaust gases (left after burning fuel). When the inlet valve is open, a mixture of air and gasoline enters the cylinder, and the piston moves up, compressing the mixture. The gasoline is ignited by a spark from

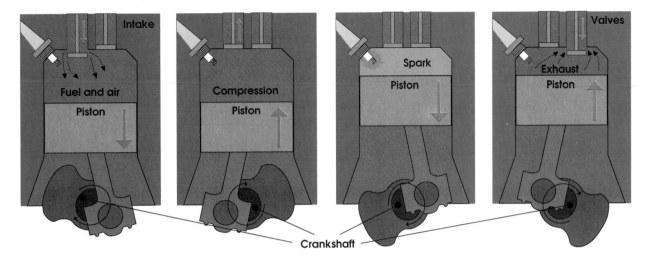

Intake

Fuel and air

Piston

Compression

Piston

Spark

Piston

Valves

Exhaust

Piston

Crankshaft

a spark plug. The explosion forces the piston downward, moving rods connected to the wheels. The fumes from the burned gasoline escape through the exhaust valve. Then the piston rises, and the process begins again.

The movement of the pistons powers the engine. Cars can have 4, 6, 8, or even 12 pistons that work in sequence. Two-cylinder cars are sometimes built.

Another kind of engine is widely used in trucks and industry. The diesel engine has no spark plug. Instead, it compresses air so much that it heats enough to explode when the fuel is injected into the cylinder. Diesel fuel does not have to be as highly refined as gasoline and it costs less.

Autos Multiply. Before long, most American families had at least one car. Miles and miles of roads were built to accommodate all the vehicles, and people hit the highways in great numbers. They took longer trips, and demanded more gasoline. Oil-producing and refining companies struggled to meet the need, pumping more from their wells and

The four movements of the piston within the cylinder of a four-stroke cycle, or internal combustion, engine.

expanding refineries to boost gasoline production.

Before gasoline stations became common in the United States, people got their gasoline from a place called a bulk plant, where they purchased it in 5- and 10-gallon (18- and 38-liter) containers. In areas far from a bulk plant, gasoline was transported by a tank car on a train. When the fuel reached its destination, it was stored close to the train tracks in smaller tanks owned by the oil company. Distributors sold it from there. People brought in their own containers to fill, and then took them home for storage.

The first gasoline station in the United States was developed by a man in Los Angeles, California, around 1920. He bought a tanker truck full of gasoline, attached a hose and nozzle, and parked it on a busy corner. His business was a wild success. Soon, permanent stations, offering auto maintenance and other services, were built.

Cities began to spread out into suburbs as workers moved away from crowded downtown areas. People preferred to live where there was enough space to have larger houses with lawns, and they used their cars to go into the city to work.

When cars became popular, businesses sprang up to meet the needs of motorists. The gas station below offered fuel, changed flat tires, and performed other repair work.

As cars take over the roads and highways take over the land, our air becomes more and more filled with the pollution from car exhaust.

Gasoline costs much more in Europe and Japan than in the United States because of the taxes that are added to the price. Many countries charge $3.00 or more per gallon (3.8 liters). The governments set the prices high not only to raise money but also to make people think twice before using their cars. In China there has never been much gasoline available. Most people in Africa, Latin America, and China walk, ride bicycles, or use buses or trains instead of driving cars.

FACT

Polluting Exhaust. The main problem with cars is that they produce exhaust. The gasoline that is sparked in the cylinder contains hydrocarbons. As they burn, the hydrocarbons are chemically changed. The process gives off carbon dioxide (CO_2) as well as such dangerous pollutants as carbon monoxide (CO), nitric oxide (NO), and nitrogen dioxide (NO_2), along with some unburned and partially burned fuel. The NO and NO_2 are often called nitrogen oxides (NO_x). The average American car pumps its own weight in carbon into the atmosphere each year.

29

Harmful gas vapors are released into the atmosphere every time someone fills a car tank with gasoline. The process also allows some of the toxic liquid to drip onto the ground.

In addition, lead used to be released into the air when gasoline burned. Lead was added to gasoline to keep motors from knocking—making a rattling sound when fuel did not burn completely. The lead helped stop knocking, but when the poisonous lead fumes were inhaled, they entered the bloodstream. Lead poisoning causes convulsions, severe vomiting, cramps, and brain damage. Leaded gasoline has been banned for sale in the United States.

Gasoline Vapors. Adding to pollution is the amount of gasoline that evaporates when it is moved from one container to another. Imagine how much goes into the atmosphere when a tanker truck is originally filled, then again when the truck pours its contents into the gas station's underground tank, and yet again when we fill the tanks of our cars. You've probably smelled gasoline fumes when your car is being filled, or even seen the vapors—they resemble heat shimmering in the air.

Dirty Industry

During Joseph Stalin's rule of the Soviet Union from 1929 to 1953, and after the Communist takeover in China in October 1949, both countries increased their industrial output. Steel mills and other factories were built, often quickly, cheaply, and without thought for the future. All of them used coal because it was inexpensive and easy to get.

The steel mills and other industries provided jobs needed by the people. But today, these factories are nearly worthless, producing low-grade products and belching toxic smoke into the sky. The nearby towns are dirty and their water is polluted. Replacing the factories or modernizing them is very expensive. But until these factories are replaced or shut down, they will continue to pump out pollutants.

Much the same thing happened in China. Wanting to modernize, the government began building factories, which were supposed to make China more independent. Again, many of these were steel mills and other heavy industries fueled by coal. Now China is facing the same problem as the Soviet republics. They must either shut down the plants, even though they can't afford to build new ones, or continue making inferior products and polluting the atmosphere.

The Berlin Wall separated democratic western Germany from its communist East German neighbor for almost thirty years. When the wall came down in 1990, East Germany's steel mills were found to be major polluters. It will take millions of dollars and many years to fix them.

In most countries, factories built before the 1970s were

The iron and steel industries throughout the world are big users of coal. Much of it is burned to generate heat to process the metals, and large amounts of dangerous emissions are released into the air we breathe.

31

not very efficient. Fuel was cheap, and so no thought was given to burning it thoroughly. Coal smoke poured out of steel mills, auto-assembly plants, and electrical power plants. If people complained about the emissions (smoke, toxic gases, and particles of solid matter), companies built smokestacks taller so the fumes went higher into the atmosphere. The pollutants were carried away by the winds. But they then landed in someone else's backyard.

The Demand Continues

Signs of impending trouble from fossil-fuel use have been impossible to ignore as the years have passed. The Earth suffers from coal-smoke pollution mixed with the exhaust emissions from millions of cars. Still, inhabitants of the planet continue to demand more energy.

Electricity Production. Large amounts of fossil fuels are used by power plants to produce electricity. Electrical power is measured in units called watts. The name comes from Scottish inventor James Watt, who perfected steam power in 1769. You may have seen the word on a light bulb. A kilowatt is 1,000 watts, and a megawatt is 1 million watts. The amount of energy used in a home is measured in kilowatt-hours (kwh). A kilowatt-hour is the power in kilowatts, multiplied by the number of hours the power is used.

To produce electricity, coal is burned to heat water. This creates steam, which is used to turn turbines—large wheels of blades on a rod, rather like a propeller. The turning rod is attached to the generator. The generator houses a magnet that spins inside a ring wrapped with wire. Magnetic fields rotate within the ring, and this produces electric current in the wire.

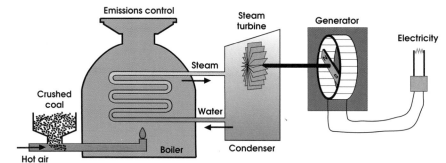

To get an idea of how much power a kilowatt is, think of how much television your family watches in a month. It takes about 30 to 50 kilowatt-hours to run the average television set that long. Your washing machine uses nearly 13 kilowatt-hours of energy to wash eight loads of clothes.

Making Electricity

Magnetism and electricity go together. Generators are constructed with this in mind. Power companies use gas, gasoline, water, nuclear energy, or wind turbines to turn the generators that make electricity. The following experiment demonstrates how an electric current is produced.

Borrow a galvanometer from a junior high school laboratory. (A galvanometer is a device that detects small electric currents.) The movement of the galvanometer's needle in one direction or the other indicates the direction of the current. Most power plants supply alternating current to houses and industries. Alternating current rapidly changes direction and usually can't be detected on a galvanometer unless the instrument is put on the "AC" setting.

Purchase about 15 feet (4.5 meters) of bell wire and a bar magnet. Wrap the wire around a metal can or cardboard cylinder, leaving the ends long enough to attach to the galvanometer. Slip the coil of wire off the container. The insulation on the last inch (2.5 centimeters) of wire should be stripped off where the bare wire is wrapped around each post (see the illustration).

Move the bar magnet in and out of the wire coil. As you do, note the movement and direction of the needle. When you hold the magnet still in the coil, is a current produced?

The demand for fossil fuels is growing around the world. Even in a remote area of Liberia, a gas station serves the needs of drivers.

Popular Fossil Fuels. Coal supplies one-third of the energy used by people throughout the world, but coal has other uses, too.

Many different products are made from coal. Chemicals, coal tar, and a light oil called coke oven crude are used daily by businesses and industries. Chemical products made from coal include dyes, waxes, drugs, and pesticides.

The demand for oil is also huge. Breaking oil into its component parts and rearranging its molecules gives us gasoline, kerosene, plastics, such textiles as polyester and nylon, photographic film, lubricants, jet fuel, butane, propylene, butylene, waxes, and solvents, which are substances that break down or dissolve other substances.

Natural gas leaves no ash and produces much less pollution than other fuels when it is burned. Because of this, natural gas is favored for heating houses and businesses, for industrial uses, and for generating electricity. It can also be used to power cars and trucks, but as yet few vehicles are equipped to use it.

Fossil fuels are non-renewable—as they are used up, they cannot be replaced. If their use is not slowed or stopped, the world will eventually use up all its oil, gas, and coal. Some experts predict this will happen with coal by the year 2260. The U.S. Department of Energy estimates that only slightly more than 60 years' supply of natural gas is still in reserve.

If the rest of the world used fossil fuels at the same per capita (for each person) rate as the United States does, we would run out of oil and gas within the next 15 years. The United States uses more energy per person than most other countries, but the fuel comes from all over the world.

Our Poisoned Earth

The problems we encounter from using fossil fuels are well known. Burning them causes such serious problems as acid rain and other air pollution and global warming.

As smoke continues to pour from factories and cars, metropolitan areas like Los Angeles, Saõ Paulo in Brazil, and Mexico City, have been immersed for days at a time under an ugly yellow blanket of choking smog.

When sulfur emissions from coal-powered industries mix with water vapor in the air, they turn to sulfuric acid and fall to the Earth as acid rain. Acid rain apparently destroys trees and kills plant and animal life in ponds and lakes. It can even eat holes in brick and stone. Acid rain was first detected in the northern United States and southern Canada during the 1960s. It has damaged statues and buildings in Rome, London, and Moscow. It has seriously damaged forests in Poland, Germany, Canada, and the United States.

When acid rain falls to Earth, it causes serious damage. Statues and monuments, such as the Civil War Memorial below, deteriorate, and many trees are weakened and die (right) *due to the acid in the rain.*

Ash left from burning coal is also difficult to get rid of because it is highly acidic from the high sulfur content in the coal. If spread on the ground, the ash will quickly cause the soil to become so acidified that nothing will grow.

Mining, especially strip mining, is ugly and dangerous, and it pollutes groundwater. Oil wells can pollute nearby streams and lakes, even underground water, from leaking pipes. Oil spills can cause tremendous environmental harm.

An oil-pipe leak in the Chesapeake Bay area in 1991 fouled several harbors and hurt wildlife in a nearby wetland. Spills like the 1989 *Exxon Valdez* disaster in Alaska can ruin fish spawning grounds and create hardship for fishermen. Oil spills at sea mean death for thousands of sea creatures.

Our weather, too, may be affected by fossil fuels, through the process called *global warming*. The Earth's average temperatures have grown warmer, possibly as a result of a boosting of the greenhouse effect. Such gases as methane and carbon dioxide build up in the atmosphere and trap more heat than usual. Scientists predict that future warming will almost certainly occur if this buildup is not stopped.

Fossil fuels have helped many industries around the world to become profitable and to support workers. But does that justify the pollution fossil fuels cause? Many people think there must be ways to power our industries that are better for the Earth.

Such warming could give Boston the same warm climate as Washington, DC, and it could give Washington, DC, the climate of Houston. It could also kill plants, change the areas of the world where crops can grow, and cause sea levels to rise as the ocean warms and expands. You'll learn more about global warming in the next chapter.

For years, a few environmentally conscious people tried to warn the rest of the world of the dangers to our whole planet that could come from our dependence on fossil fuels. The damage has now become impossible to ignore, and many more of us have accepted the fact that fossil fuels are to blame. It is time to act.

When the Exxon Valdez *ripped its hull on rocks off the coast of Alaska, it released thousands of barrels of oil. The pollution was enormous, and many sea and land creatures and plants were killed. It will take many years for nature to restore the area completely.*

Chapter 3

Environmental
Action

AS THE USE OF FOSSIL FUELS increased in the mid-1900s, so did the pollution it caused. People began to recognize the problems caused by all the smoke and exhaust fumes. They started to pressure their governments to take action.

The British were among the first to take active measures against pollution. The government passed a Clean Air Bill after the killer fog of 1952. It cracked down on pollutants such as industrial coal smoke and auto emissions. It also banned coal burning in London houses.

The United States finally passed its own Clean Air Act in 1970. The act set guidelines for reducing sulfur oxides, carbon monoxide, particulates, and lead. However, few people —and even fewer industries—took serious steps toward energy efficiency until the crisis of 1973.

The Fuel Crisis

In the mid-1960s and early 1970s, more cheap oil from Saudi Arabia, Kuwait, and Iran was imported into Western countries than was pumped from Western wells. Oil companies in the United States, Europe, and elsewhere found it difficult to compete. Many went bankrupt.

But in 1973, the flood of oil shipped out of the Middle East to industrialized nations suddenly stopped. Disagreements flared between the Organization of Petroleum Exporting Countries (OPEC), which controlled the supply and the price of oil, and several Western countries. OPEC's members stopped shipping so much oil.

Gasoline prices doubled in less than a month. Long lines of cars waited at gasoline pumps. Signs on gas stations read "SORRY, NO GAS."

When oil shipments to the United States from the Middle East were stopped in the 1970s, many gasoline stations were forced to close each time they ran out of fuel. Those that still had gasoline to sell were swamped by drivers that wanted to fill their cars' tanks.

The Energy Crunch. For the first time since World War II, the United States urged its citizens to conserve energy. People set their thermostats between 68 and 72 degrees F. (20 and 22.2 degrees C) in winter, and at 80 to 82 degrees F. (26.7 to 27.8 degrees C) in summer. Highway speed limits were dropped from 65 to 55 miles (105 to 88.5 kilometers) per hour—the top speed at which a car could use gas efficiently. Daylight Saving Time became the norm everywhere except in Arizona to take advantage of most daylight hours. Many people bought smaller, more fuel-efficient cars. The government passed regulations requiring automakers to meet certain standards of energy efficiency.

Scientists and engineers rushed to find ways to conserve energy: better insulation for buildings, more efficient lights and light bulbs. They looked for ways to burn coal more thoroughly with less emissions. Wind turbines and solar panels—which create energy from the wind and the sun— were improved. The U.S. government gave tax breaks to people who used such alternative sources of energy.

Canadian Oil. Canada was one of the few countries in good shape. The western provinces had large petroleum reserves. Companies sank new wells and began mining oil shale—a type of rock that soaks up oil formed around it. The long waits at gas stations, rising prices, and "NO GAS" signs common in the United States were unknown in Canada. But the nation experienced other problems.

Since the eastern, most populated, section of Canada demanded and consumed most of the fuel produced in the west, bad feelings were created. Trade between eastern and western provinces is still affected by the distrust that started in the 1970s.

Tightening Down. Part of the solution to the shortage of gasoline was an increase in oil production in the United States. The other part was conservation. The combination worked.

The scarcity of oil persuaded local prospectors to hunt for "black gold" in North America again. Many oil wells, abandoned because they could not produce petroleum at competitive prices, were reopened. New techniques were developed to make oil wells more effective. One of these methods, steam injection, is a process that brings oil to the surface by forcing high-pressure steam into the well.

Oil mining became popular again. This is a procedure in which petroleum-saturated sandstone is blasted or drilled out, then processed to release the oil. It had not been used since the industry's early days because there was a great

The reduction in oil shipments from the Middle East forced Americans to consider alternative sources of energy. The use of wind turbines, like those shown above, became more popular.

deal of easily pumped liquid oil available.

People also converted their home heating systems from more expensive, hard-to-get fuel oil to natural gas. Alternative energy sources, which used the sun, wind, and water, were improved and used more frequently.

When people realized that oil was going to be in short supply for an unknown period of time, they buckled down to the sometimes uncomfortable task of conserving fuel. Conservation, in some cases, meant more discomfort, because air-conditioning settings were higher and heat settings were lower. But the United States and other countries responded, proving that little things could make differences in energy consumption. Joy-riding in cars went down, saving gasoline. Most people used their cars only when they had to. Buses and subways gained riders. Businesses were very careful about heating, cooling, and other energy uses. Many homeowners insulated their houses. People tended to think much more about using energy.

Conservation also produced an explosion in technology. Laboratories, universities, and research centers around the

An Earth Experience

Burning Oil

These experiments will help show how burning fossil fuels produces carbon dioxide, which contributes to global warming.

Use a ball of modeling clay to hold a short candle upright in the middle of a metal pan with a rim. Set a 1-quart (1-liter) glass jar upside down over the candle. In a short time the candle goes out. What does the fire need in air? Why didn't the flame go out immediately?

world came out with new designs for machines and products meant to increase efficiency. For instance, smaller cars became popular because they used less fuel. Fluorescent light bulbs replaced incandescent bulbs because they produce a greater amount of light with less electricity.

Industries began producing double-glazed windows for houses. These have two pieces of glass in each window frame. The panes are separated by air, which doesn't allow heat to escape or cold to enter as easily as plain glass. Many sources of alternative energy were investigated.

Global Warming

Scientists have long known that certain gases in the atmosphere trap the sun's heat. Short-wave radiation from the sun passes through the atmosphere and strikes the ground. Re-emitted as longer-wave heat radiation, it is trapped by water vapor, carbon dioxide, and other gases in the atmosphere. This process is called the *greenhouse effect*. Without it, Earth would not be warm and habitable.

However, at the end of the 1800s, Svante Arrhenius of

With an adult present, light a match and hold it near the mouth of the upside-down jar. Tilt the jar slightly to let the gases inside it pour out toward the flame. What happens? Did water vapor condense in droplets on the inside of the jar?

Candle wax contains carbon and hydrogen, the same elements that make up the hydrocarbons in coal and oil. The hydrogen combined with oxygen to form water inside the jar. When wax burns, the carbon given off combines with oxygen in the air to form carbon dioxide, a major contributor to global warming.

Sweden and Thomas C. Chamberlain of the United States published their idea that the Earth's temperature might be rising beyond normal limits faster than it ever had before. This temperature rise became known as *global warming*.

During the 1970s, scientists began gathering temperature records and comparing them with old documents to study temperature rise. Other measurements show that the amount of CO_2 in the atmosphere is steadily rising and is now about 30 percent higher than before fossil fuels were widely used. Some scientists believe this shows evidence of global warming caused by the rise in CO_2 and other gases.

But others believe that the warming is simply part of our planet's natural cycle of cooling and heating, and that we don't need to worry. A recent study shows average world temperatures have increased between 0.9 and 1.26 degrees F. (0.5 and 0.7 degrees C) since 1860. Until more evidence is in, no firm judgment can be made. But the question is, can we take the risk that global warming is *not* real?

The Dangers of Global Warming. On a cold winter day, global warming may sound pleasant—until you consider the problems it would cause. The seas would get warmer and expand, causing ocean levels to rise and swamp low-lying areas. Areas like southern Louisiana; Venice, Italy; southern Florida; and Bangladesh would disappear. Some areas would have to build dikes and pumping systems the way the Netherlands did. Much of that nation's land is below sea level and requires constant effort to avoid flooding.

Global warming also could have serious effects on food crops. Central North America, where much of the world's food is grown, would probably become hotter and drier,

Global warming, caused in part by the burning of fossil fuels, may cause the ocean water to warm and expand. This could cause the flooding of many cities, including Venice, which is already sinking.

making it more difficult to grow familiar crops. New strains might have to be developed to withstand the heat.

Some scientists and environmentalists believe that if the Earth warms another few degrees, microscopic plants called phytoplankton would die. This means famine among krill, which are tiny shrimp that feed on phytoplankton. Krill are the food for a huge number of fish and mammals, including several species of whales. There would likely be starvation all the way up the ocean's food chain.

Phytoplankton is an important link at the bottom of the ocean's food chain. Global warming could kill phytoplankton, and without it, many other ocean creatures would starve.

Coral, too, would be affected by a rise in water temperature. Small marine animals called polyps build hard shelters for themselves in tropical waters. Each generation adds to the hard part, called coral. After thousands of years, the coral clusters become reefs—ridges of coral near the water's surface—or atolls, which are islands made of coral.

Warmer weather would change the growth patterns of coral, and may even kill the polyps. The world would lose an unusual animal, one that is an essential element of tropical island building.

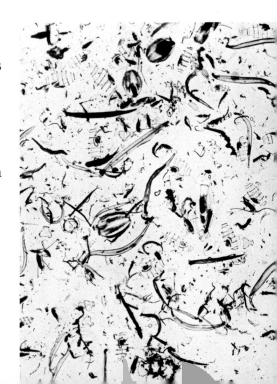

Burning Wood

In a process called photosynthesis, green plants use the energy in sunlight to change carbon dioxide and water to make sugars, such as glucose, cellulose, and others. Light energy is changed during that process into various kinds of chemical energy. A tree is loaded with carbon, hydrogen, and oxygen. When wood is burned these elements are released. They combine to form carbon dioxide (CO_2) and water (H_2O). This experiment will help you understand the different chemicals that get into the air when things burn.

Find a glass jar with a tight cover. Put it in the freezer to let it chill. After an hour, remove the jar. With the help of an adult, light two or three small pieces of wood—wooden matches will work. Quickly drop them into the cold jar and cap it. What collects on the inside of the jar?

When the wood stops burning, use potholders to remove the lid and quickly pour in a tablespoon of water mixed with lime. You can get lime from a garden shop. Quickly replace the lid. Shake gently, mixing the limewater and the air in the jar. Does the liquid change color? If carbon dioxide is present, limewater turns milky.

Correcting Our Mistakes

If people continue to use fossil fuels at the present rate, the world can look forward to continued global warming as well as health problems related to pollution. Action must be taken to correct our mistakes or the planet Earth might soon become too warm to live on.

Cars Clean Up. Engineers, inventors, and scientists have introduced new technology to reduce pollutants and increase efficiency in vehicles, industries, and homes. When unleaded gasoline became common in the 1980s, lead in the atmosphere was reduced by 48 percent. The total drop since then has been 90 percent.

During the 1980s, an appliance called a catalytic converter became a required part of most new cars. This device removes pollutants from the exhaust system. It filters hot gases such as unburned hydrocarbons and carbon monoxide coming out of tailpipes. A honeycomb of beads coated with platinum and palladium inside the converter allows fewer toxic emissions such as nitrogen oxides and carbon monoxide to escape. The converter has helped reduce atmospheric pollutants, but more needs to be done about pollution from automobiles.

Some new small cars can average 57 to 60 miles per gallon (23 to 25 kilometers per liter) of gasoline because of better designs, stronger and lighter materials, and more fuel-efficient engines.

New, more aerodynamic designs, with fewer places where airflow over the body is stopped by squared corners and parts that stick out, have also added to the energy efficiency of vehicles. You may have seen large cargo trucks going down the highway with an odd-looking fiberglass hood on top of the cab. This addition creates a smoother line from the windshield up over the front of the trailer. Less air resistance means greater fuel efficiency.

Studies have shown that on airplanes, too, each bolt exposed on a wing or the fuselage adds wind resistance and increases fuel usage. Modern planes have bolts set even with the body, and future airplanes will use hidden bolts. New metals and paints also create less wind resistance.

A new variation of fuel is *compressed natural gas*—natural gas that has been squeezed under high pressure. It is more efficient and less expensive than gasoline. Trucks and some school buses are being converted. Several compressed gas stations have opened in widely scattered areas of the United States to fuel them. More such stations are planned.

Trade-Offs

It often happens that the methods used to prevent one kind of environmental problem cause damage in some other way. People trying to solve the problem must then decide which is worse—the original harm, or the new one. This is called a trade-off.

Unfortunately, trade-offs are common in efforts to save the environment. We will encounter several examples of trade-offs throughout the rest of this book. As you read about each one, take the time to think about it. What choice would you make?

FACT

Today, the average new car in North America travels about twice as far as a new car did in 1973 on the same amount of fuel. More fuel-efficient cars save 1.51 million barrels of oil each day. In 1973, a new car averaged 14 miles per gallon (mpg) [5.8 kilometers per liter (kpl)]. Fuel efficiency rose to an average of 28.7 mpg (12 kpl) in 1988, a gain of 105 percent. But in 1990 the average mileage in the United States fell to 27.8 mpg (11.6 kpl).

Trade-Off: Gasoline vs. Electricity. Electric cars will soon be produced by at least two major American automobile manufacturers. Several auto manufacturers in Japan and

Europe are also designing electric cars. Since they don't burn fossil fuels, emission reductions in crowded, smoggy areas such as Los Angeles, Denver, the East Coast, and Toronto, Canada, will be significant.

But what happens when everyone with an electric car gets home at night? They plug their cars into electric sockets to recharge. Since most generating plants are fueled by coal or gas, more fossil fuel will be burned to provide energy for the electric cars. Also, rechargeable batteries have a limited lifetime, so they end up in recycling bins and landfills.

The battery pack being installed in this electric car will replace fossil fuels as the car's source of power.

On the positive side, the power plant will be producing electricity for the new autos during off-peak times. This means the plant can run more efficiently. In addition, pollutants from one centralized power plant can be controlled more easily than pollutants from thousands of cars.

Producing Less Pollution

Today, pipelines transporting oil and natural gas are better made than older pipes, so there are far fewer cracks from which the fuel can leak and evaporate into the environment. Some oil tankers are being built with double hulls that are damaged less easily. If all oil companies use only tankers with double hulls, devastating oil spills like the *Exxon Valdez* disaster in Alaska should rarely happen.

New methods are being developed to make coal use less harmful, too. *Gasification* is a technique in which coal is made into a cleaner-burning gas. Water is added, then special

Many electricity generating plants use scrubbers to clean pollutants from the emissions produced by burning coal. In this photo, the scrubbers are seen at the base of the tall smokestack.

combustion processes are used. Less pollution is produced when the gas is burned than when the coal is burned.

Another procedure that is being cleaned up is the manufacture of *petrochemicals*. These chemicals are made from petroleum that has been broken down by heating and processing—methods that require tremendous amounts of energy. The chemicals include ethylene, propylene, benzene, plastics, solvents, and synthetic fibers. The use of cleaner-burning fuels is being experimented with. Special filters capture toxic by-products. These are refined into usable chemicals and sold to other businesses.

Trade-Off: Cleanup vs. Coal Use. An increasing number of industries that burn coal are turning to scrubbers to help clean up their emissions. Scrubbers are smokestack cleaners that can remove 90 percent of the sulfur from power-plant and industrial smoke.

But scrubbers are expensive—about $25 million for one set of smokestacks. And in order to power the scrubbers, generating plants must burn more coal. Scrubbers use a great deal of power and produce a great deal of waste.

Cogeneration

Some companies are using materials or heat left over from their manufacturing processes to produce electricity. This is called cogeneration.

One such company is Marriott New Jersey Textile in Edison, New Jersey. Once just a laundry, the company now produces 60 percent of the electricity it needs. A heating plant was added that raises the temperature of wastewater by 35 degrees F. (17 degrees C) and runs it through turbines to produce electricity. The business now buys less power and uses less natural gas to heat water.

More cogeneration projects are taking place in Canada, where many forest-industry plants have built their own electrical generators. Paper mills cut fuel costs by using waste heat to produce power.

Other businesses using cogeneration include oil-recovery projects where steam is injected into the ground to force thick petroleum to the surface. After petroleum is pumped to the surface, the water is separated from it, cleaned, and then used to heat buildings or turn turbines.

Sometimes two neighboring companies work together on a cogeneration project. For example, suppose an electric

One example of cogeneration might occur in a food-processing plant. Coal is used to boil water in which vegetables are cooked. Steam is piped off from the vegetables to turn the blades of a turbine. This enables a generator to produce electricity that helps power the plant. The steam, meanwhile, condenses into water and is once again used for cooking.

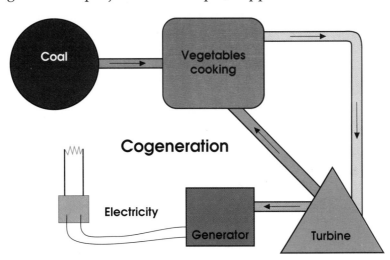

plant produces steam that is usually wasted. A vegetable-processing plant built next door can use that same steam to cook canned vegetables. With careful regional planning, a lot of fossil fuel could be saved by cogeneration projects.

Smart Controls

No matter how plentiful or efficient energy sources are, it makes no sense to waste them. Typical heating and air-conditioning controls in commercial buildings keep temperatures comfortable whether anyone is in the building or not.

In a computerized management system, sensors are installed throughout an old building or built into new ones. A computer collects information from the sensors, matches the readings against ideal conditions for comfort and efficiency, and makes adjustments in the equipment.

Individuals can still make adjustments. If you wanted your office temperature at 74 degrees F. (23 degrees C), the

Though city lights are beautiful, they waste a lot of electricity lighting empty rooms. Smart controls would correct the problem by automatically shutting off office lights when the last occupant leaves.

system would keep it there. If you wanted it to be at 65 degrees F. (18 degrees C) tomorrow, you would simply type a command into your computer.

The sensors respond to temperature, hazardous gases, humidity, motion, or lights. They can have the computer turn off the lights when a person leaves an office and turn them on again when he or she returns. They also warn the people in charge when something is wrong in the system.

With all this conservation and increasing efficiency, it might seem as if we're doing enough to keep the world from death by pollution. Not so. The population of the world is increasing rapidly. Developing countries are building industries that require energy sources.

The answer lies in finding other sources of energy. There will be little additional real progress in saving Earth from death by pollution until we begin to use other, cleaner sources of energy.

As the world's demand for electricity continues to grow, we must also cut our dependence on fossil fuels. It's important that we find other ways to meet our energy needs.

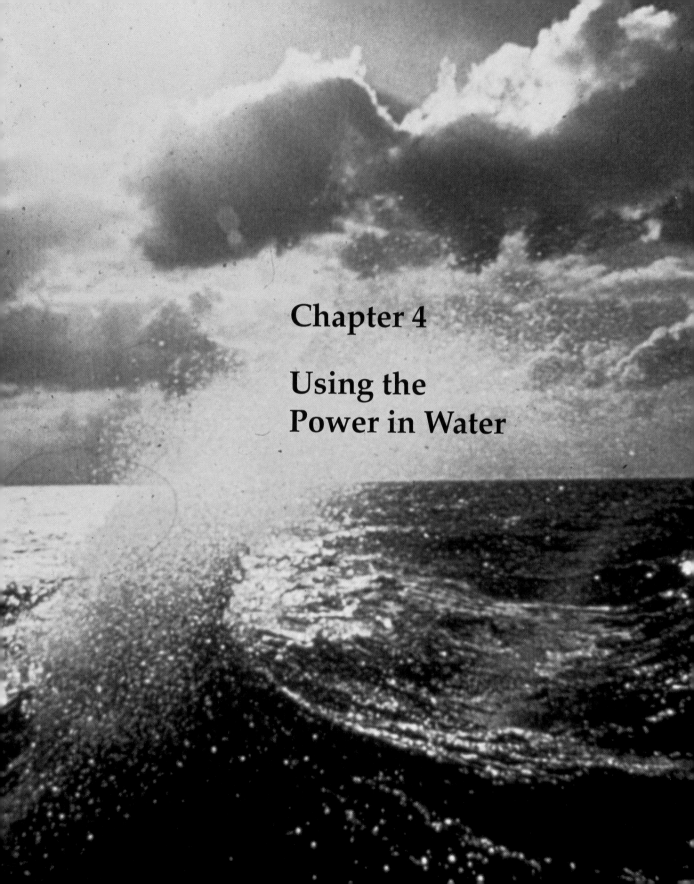

Chapter 4

Using the
Power in Water

WATER IS VITAL TO LIFE ON EARTH. It also provides an energy source that helps us continue to live on this planet.

Since the 1890s, when the practical electric motor was invented and electric light became common in homes, the main source of energy to make electricity has been fossil fuels. Most research into other ways to fuel the future without harming the Earth still involve electricity. One of the primary ways puts water to work.

For centuries people have been using waterwheels and dams to power mills to grind flour, forges to bend steel, and run other small industries. Today, water power is still important in poor, developing countries that may not have other resources.

Hydroelectric Power

Electricity is generated (produced) when a turbine is turned and it moves electromagnets through a coil of wire. The turning motion creates (induces) an electric charge in the coil. The mechanical energy of the turning motion is changed into electrical energy. Fossil fuels are usually used to produce the steam that turns the turbine. But the force of water can also turn the blades on a turbine. Such use of water is called hydroelectric power (*hydro* means "water").

Hydroelectric power is usually created by building a dam that backs the water in a river up until it creates a great deal of pressure. When water is released from the lake, or *reservoir*, behind the dam, it falls with great force, causing a turbine to spin and sending mechanical energy into the generator. The electrical energy created is sent out to homes and businesses through wires.

Energy from Falling Water

With an adult's help, drill a hole the exact diameter of a wooden dowel rod through the center of a circle of plywood. The plywood should be 3/4 inch (19 millimeters) thick and 12 inches (30 centimeters) in diameter. Using strong waterproof tape or glue, fasten six or eight small juice cans to the outside of the circle of plywood. The open ends of the cans should all be facing the same direction. Spacing between cans should be equal. Construct a wooden stand to hold the wheel and axle.

Force the dowel through the center of the wheel. It should be very tight—when the wheel turns, the dowel-axle should also turn. Make holes in the supports of the stand large enough so the dowel is free to turn easily. Nail a small piece of wood on each end of the dowel to keep it from slipping out.

Use a garden hose as your source of falling water. Fill one can on the wheel with water. The weight of the water will make the wheel start to turn. An empty can will come into range of your hose and will, in turn, fill, causing the wheel to keep turning.

If an electrical generator were attached to this water-powered wheel, you could make a little electricity.

The Itaipu Dam on the Paraná River between Brazil and Paraguay is the largest hydroelectric plant in the world. Completed in 1982, it generates 12,600 megawatts of power each year.

Construction of dams hit a low point in the late 1960s and early 1970s when oil was plentiful. After the oil crisis, hydroelectric projects were started all over the world. Today, 20 percent of the world's electricity needs are supplied by hydroelectric power. Hydroelectric generation produces 10 percent of the total energy used in the United States.

Trade-Off: Power vs. Land. Even though dams seem to be an excellent source of nonpolluting electricity, there are trade-offs. When a large dam is built, the water in the reservoir may flood thousands of acres of land. This often boosts recreation and brings tourists into the area. But families have been forced to move, wildlife has been drowned or driven away, and natural formations such as wind-carved rocks have been buried underwater.

During construction of the Aswan High Dam on the Nile River in Egypt during the 1960s, a temple thousands of years old, called Abu Simbel, had to be moved. Shortly before the site was flooded by the new Lake Nasser, archeologists, engineers, and scientists took the temple apart, numbered its pieces, moved them to safety, and then reconstructed the temple. Other artifacts were impossible to save, however, and 90,000 Egyptians and Sudanese nomads who lived in the valley had to move.

The Aswan High Dam generated 2,100 megawatts of power each year after it was completed in 1971. But the project has had more bad effects than good. The fertile Nile

Delta north of Cairo is disappearing because new sediment is no longer deposited there. Farmers once relied on the Nile's annual floods to deposit fertile silt on their fields. When the dam stopped the flooding, crop production dropped. Now the river drops silt in front of the dam, so electrical production has also dropped because the water cannot flow as well. The environmental costs of this dam have been very high.

Water is an inexhaustible resource—it is replaced by melting snow and rain, which run into the river or the reservoir behind the dam. But building a dam takes a tremendous investment, especially the purchase of land. Dams were once thought to have a low environmental impact, but we now know that isn't true. These financial and environmental factors have made costs for hydroelectricity match those of fossil-fuel generators.

Projects Big and Little

Dams are not the only source of hydroelectric power. The Niagara River thunders between Lake Erie and Lake Ontario, forming the world-famous Niagara Falls. There is a unique two-part hydroelectric generating system on the United States side of the falls. The water intakes for the Robert Moses Niagara Power Project are 2.5 miles (4 kilometers) above the falls, but the power plant is 5 miles (8 kilometers) below. Twin pipes 66 feet (20 meters) high and 46 feet wide (14 meters) run 4.5 miles (7.2 kilometers) underground to a man-made river called a forebay. The water then drops 305 feet (93 meters). The power of the falling water turns the turbines to create energy.

The second part of the process takes place at the nearby

When a dam is built on a river, the river backs up to form a lake. One of the largest of these lakes is Lake Mead (below), created when the Hoover Dam was built on the Colorado River at the Arizona-Nevada border. Near most dams are powerhouses containing generators. The houses above are the Big Creek Powerhouses in California. Generators (below, right) convert energy from a dam's flowing water into electrical energy. The generators shown are part of a hydroelectric complex that supplies 70 percent of Kenya's electricity.

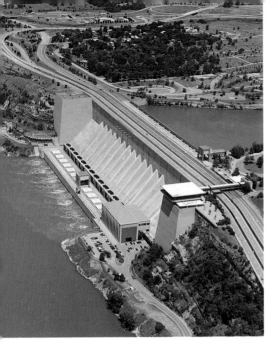

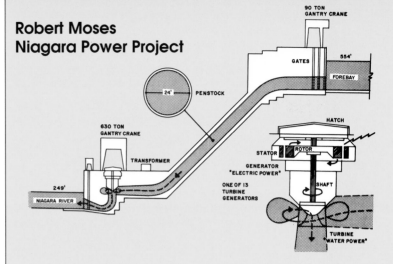

The Robert Moses Niagara Power Project (left) *takes water from the Niagara River and guides it through a series of pipes. The water drops onto turbines that spin generators to produce electricity.*

Lewiston Pump Generating Station. At night, water is pumped from the Niagara into a reservoir and held until morning when energy demand rises. The pumps are reversed and become generators as water from the reservoir is released. The water joins water going to the Robert Moses plant. It is used a second time to generate electricity there.

A treaty signed by Canada and the United States allows both countries to generate energy from the river. It guarantees that half the normal volume of water is allowed to go over Niagara Falls during the day so that the falls still look spectacular to visitors. During the night and throughout the winter, the generating stations get to use three-quarters of the river's volume of water.

The Niagara Power Project is testing a new turbine that may boost energy output by about 15 percent. If it does well, all the turbines will be replaced within seven years.

The James Bay Project. Quebec, the French-speaking province of Canada, has begun the impressive James Bay hydroelectric project. Three major rivers and several streams have been turned to run through 41 miles (66 kilometers) of dams. Three powerhouses contain 37 turbines which equal the output of approximately 28 nuclear power plants or 60 coal-fired plants. Canada sells part of this electricity to the United States. These sales represent about 5 percent of the electricity demand in the New England states.

But the James Bay project is not being built without problems. Changing river courses has altered important spawning grounds—areas where fish reproduce—and partially drained some streams. Large areas have been flooded to create five reservoirs, more than half the size of Lake Ontario. Some 11,000 Cree Indians and 6,000 Inuit live in Northern Quebec. Development has brought improved health and social conditions, but has also disturbed their traditional hunting, fishing, and trapping grounds. The challenge in Quebec since development began has been to enable modern and traditional economies to thrive beside each other.

Hydro-Quebec, the project's sponsor, claims that the environmental impacts of construction and operation of the dams can be predicted and managed. Others disagree. Do you think it is all right to change the environment and disrupt the lives of some people for what seems an endless, profitable, nonpolluting energy source that will benefit many others?

The James Bay hydroelectric project in Quebec produces enormous amounts of electricity through a series of dams. Reservoirs created by the dams have flooded a large area.

Dams are costly to build and can cause the loss of valuable land areas. But because they are a source of practically pollution-free energy, many countries continue building dams to produce electricity.

Mini and Micro Hydro. A hunting lodge sits beside a rushing trout stream deep in a Canadian forest. There are no power lines running to it—they are too expensive for either the owner of the lodge or the province's government to put in. Yet food is cooking, lights are on, and someone is using a washing machine. Where is the electricity coming from? From their own generator, located in a shed beside the stream.

Such small dams and generators are known as mini or micro hydroelectric projects. They are often the only practical way to get power to remote areas. Many were installed after the energy crunch of the 1970s and are owned by individuals, families, or small companies.

Tidal Power

Tides are the daily movements of large bodies of water caused by the attraction of the sun and moon on the rotating Earth. They bring the water high up on land, and then pull it back offshore each day. Tides have a regular schedule, but they can be greatly affected by seasons and storms. A hurricane, for example, can drive the sea far beyond the usual high-water mark on a beach.

Tides can be used to generate power. A dam built across a water inlet allows seawater to pour through it during the rising tide and flow back out as the tide recedes. Special turbines turn in two directions to take advantage of both incoming and outgoing water.

Tidal power projects can't be built on just any coast. The dam must usually be built across an inlet or bay with tides that rise higher than average. The amount of electricity they generate depends on the water depth and the size of the bay behind the dam. The higher the tide and the larger the bay, the more power can be generated. Seasons also affect energy production. Less is produced in winter and late fall, when the sun's pull on the tides is not as strong. That means that a large community using tidal power must have a backup system.

Tidal generating systems produce energy in China, Norway, the Soviet republics, Great Britain, the United States, Canada, Argentina, and the Cambridge Gulf of western Australia.

An experimental project was launched near the town of St. Malo in Brittany, France, in 1967. Studies had been done on the 33-foot (10-meter) tides of the region for years. The result of the experiment is the Rance River Project, the most successful tidal power system in the world. The dam produces most of the power needed by a community of over 46,000 people.

Trade-Off: Tidal Power vs. Sea Life. In 1987, the possibility of building a tidal-power dam across the Bay of Fundy in Nova Scotia was studied. Tides there are the highest in the world—39 to 56 feet (12 to 17 meters) from low tide to high tide. A test dam producing 20,000 kilowatts of power was built at nearby Annapolis Royal. It has been estimated that two or three dams built in the bay could produce nearly 400 million kilowatts of energy. That's equal to the output of 250 nuclear power plants.

However, scientists did complicated computer analysis of the whole project and its possible effects on the area. They discovered that dams built across the bay might seriously affect tides hundreds of miles away in Boston and Cape Cod, Massachusetts. Even a slight change in tides along the East Coast could harm delicate sea life and injure shellfish beds already harmed by pollution and overharvesting.

There might also be changes in currents, which can turn nutrient-rich water away from areas where small fish and shellfish live. A change in tides can also increase or decrease the amount of sunlight reaching tiny organisms at the base of the food chain. If they are decreased, beds of shellfish would die, and schools of fish would seek other waters. People who fish for a living would lose their jobs.

With such serious possibilities to consider, debate over the Bay of Fundy tidal dams is still open.

Wave Power

Islay, an Irish island, takes a beating from the North Atlantic Ocean's powerful breakers almost every day. Engineers from Queens University in Belfast recently decided to take advantage of that. They built a large concrete box on a shore where waves hit hardest and most often. The seaward end of the box is partially open to waves. When water enters, air is forced from the box's first chamber into a second, which holds a turbine attached to an electric generator. The movement of the air turns the turbine. As water flows out of the first section, air rushes in to fill the space, causing the turbine to keep turning.

The machine produces 40 kilowatts, enough clean energy for the nearby town to abandon its diesel-fueled generator.

Countries bordering the stormy North Sea are well suited to wave-motion power. The European Economic Community funded research into wave power during 1991. The British government, on the other hand, decided that there was not enough energy produced from waves to make their investment in additional research worthwhile.

In Japan, lighted buoys used as navigation aids have been powered by wave action for many years. Passing waves change the air pressure around a turbine. A number of small power generators use the back-and-forth motion of waves to turn turbines.

Energy from Ocean Warmth

Ocean thermal energy conversion (OTEC) is a process suggested by French biophysicist Jacques Arsine d'Arsonval in 1881. He knew that seas and lakes have zones of different temperature, called thermoclines. These zones are warmer toward the surface where the sun strikes and colder toward the bottom. At the equator, surface seawater averages nearly 40 degrees F. (20 degrees C) warmer than it does at depths of 1,000 feet (305 meters) or more. This difference in temperature can be used to turn turbines.

One type of OTEC is called a closed-system OTEC. Because the liquids used in this system are not cheap or readily available like water, they are sealed in the pipes and used over and over. This system uses long loops of pipe that run

This open-system OTEC is located at the National Energy Laboratory of Hawaii. It uses temperature variations in the ocean water to generate energy.

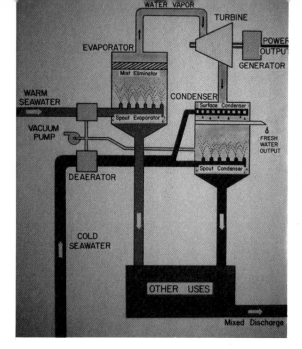

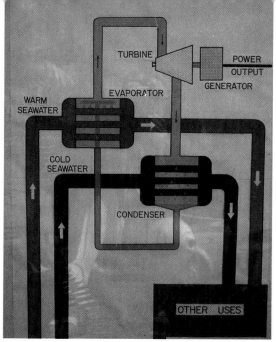

An open-system OTEC (left) vaporizes seawater with ocean warmth to create steam. The steam turns turbines that generate electricity. The water is then released back into the sea. A closed-system OTEC (right) uses pipes filled with liquid chemicals that are vaporized to turn turbines. The chemicals are then recirculated through the system.

through the thermoclines. The pipes are filled with ammonia, Freon (a chlorofluorocarbon), or propylene. These chemicals are kept at low pressure, so they boil and vaporize at lower temperatures than they would at normal pressure. The warmth in the upper layers of the sea is enough to make them turn to gas.

The vapor is routed through turbines, turning the blades, and then back into the pipes going down into the cold layers. The temperature drop condenses the gas back into liquid. This conversion occurs over and over, keeping the turbines turning.

An open-system OTEC vaporizes seawater, which is released into the ocean after use. This system also removes salt from the seawater, which can then be sold as fresh water. The third type of OTEC design is a combination of closed and open systems, using both a fluid in closed pipes and seawater.

Most sites that would be suitable for OTECs are close to the equator where there are greater differences in water temperature than in northern areas. Unfortunately, OTECs require very deep water to run properly. Also, unusual stresses on pipes, such as hurricanes and strong currents, might break them. Imagine how difficult it would be to fix a broken pipe a thousand feet under water!

Failure and Success. The first working open-system OTEC was built by French inventor Georges Claude in 1930 at Matanzas Bay, Cuba. It wasn't successful because he underestimated the energy needed to make the OTEC work. Claude also lacked modern equipment like flexible pipes. His pipes were destroyed by a storm.

The United States built an experimental OTEC in 1980, on a converted Navy ship in Pearl Harbor, Hawaii. The results were good enough to encourage more research.

The Japanese have built two successful OTECs. The first was a test plant in 1981 for the island of Nauru. Another was constructed in 1983 at Tokuno Shima. Neither was meant as a long-term facility, and both were closed within a few years, despite their success.

The most recent OTEC project is a $30-million, 40-kilowatt, onshore closed-system plant on Keahole Point in Hawaii. It is expected to produce power in 1992, but will probably run for only a short experimental period. Officials are hoping that a private electrical company will buy it when the test period is over.

One idea proposed for the use of OTECs is to construct a belt of anchored platforms around the equator. Slowly cruising converted ships are also being considered. Both of these OTECs would transfer power to the mainland or an island through a cable. They might be producing energy for places like Puerto Rico and Mexico in the next few years.

The Svartsengi geo-thermal power plant, surrounded by the Blue Lagoon, is located on the Reykjanes Peninsula in Iceland. The natural heat from within the Earth is used to generate electricity.

Energy from the Earth

Coal and oil, of course, come from the Earth, but there are sources of heat within the Earth that can be used. Geysers, for example, are natural wonders found in only a few places in the world. They provide *geothermal energy*.

Putting Geothermal to Work. Steam or hot water from an underground reservoir can be capped and controlled much like an oil well. It is run in pipes to turn nearby turbines, where it produces electricity. If a community lies close to a geothermal source, steam or hot water can be used directly for heating homes and running machinery. New Zealand, the Philippines, western South America, the western United States, Italy, Mexico, and Canada have areas where geothermal energy is available.

Geysers—one source of geothermal energy—are created when underground water strikes rock that has been heated by the molten rock deep within the Earth's center core. The water heats and expands. It gushes upward through the nearest crack, creating a geyser of steam or hot water.

A Model Steam Turbine

Follow the illustration closely to assemble the parts to make a steam turbine.

Cut a circle of heavy cardboard 8 inches (20 centimeters) in diameter. Make ten 1/2-inch (1.25-centimeter) slits around the edge to hold the blades. Cut blades 2 inches (5 centimeters) square from sturdy plastic, such as margarine tub lids. Glue the blades into the slits in a vertical position. Make a hole in the center of the wheel large enough to slip over an upside-down medicine dropper or small test tube.

Have an adult cut 6 inches (15 centimeters) of straight wire from a sturdy clothes hanger. Tape this to the side of a wooden support. It should extend enough to let the blades turn freely when you fit the dropper or test tube over the wire.

A teakettle with a curved spout set on a hot plate can be used to boil water. However, a more efficient source would be a bent glass tube in a one-hole stopper plugging the top of a laboratory flask of boiling water. Direct the steam at the blades and watch the turbine rotate.

When a generator is fastened to the turbine shaft, electricity can be produced.

The most famous geyser is Old Faithful, in Yellowstone National Park. But geysers exist elsewhere, too. In fact, the word *geyser* comes from Iceland, where geothermal energy is plentiful. Iceland heats and powers Reykjavik, its capital city, with electricity produced by geysers and other geothermal sources. El Salvador produces 40 percent of its power from geothermal sources. Nicaragua gets 28 percent of its power, and Kenya 11 percent, from geothermal sources.

Trade-Offs: Steam vs. Stench. Sometimes underground water wanders through mineral deposits, which dissolve into it. These minerals, such as sulfur, may give geothermal steam and hot water an unpleasant smell that is released when the fluids are used for power unless special controls are used. This can make an entire area smell terrible and distress nearby residents.

The minerals and salts may also clog pipes and eat holes through metal. Replacing these items can mean great expense and constant maintenance.

Another potential problem involves destruction of the

Sulfur springs, such as these in New Zealand, can be a good source of geothermal power, but can also create a terrible stench.

environment. One mining company was drilling additional geyser holes in an active field in California so that they could increase their power output. They accidentally drilled too close to the underground stream that fed them. The geysers disappeared because drill holes drained water away from their fissures. This warns us that experimenting with nature can be dangerous if not all possibilities are considered.

Power from Underground Water. A geothermal breakthrough came in 1989 when a San Diego, California, company built an unusual power plant. It taps salty water that is heated by the Earth to 600 degrees F. (316 degrees C). The water runs 3,000 to 9,000 feet (914 to 2,743 meters) beneath southern California's Imperial Valley. A previous attempt at utilizing the heat failed because the water, which is full of sand, salt, and other particles, clogged pipes when the steam passed through.

With assistance from Dow Chemical Company, Magma Power Company solved the problem. A mixture of chemicals was added to the water in the pipes to keep the salt and sand from clogging them. The power company has been producing electricity since January 1989 and has three plants functioning.

Many of these water-powered energy sources show great promise as ways to fuel our future. But if we are to truly break our dependence on fossil fuels, they are not enough, nor are they ready to take over a very significant portion of our energy use. However, it is daily becoming more important to investigate every idea that the creative minds of scientists and engineers come up with.

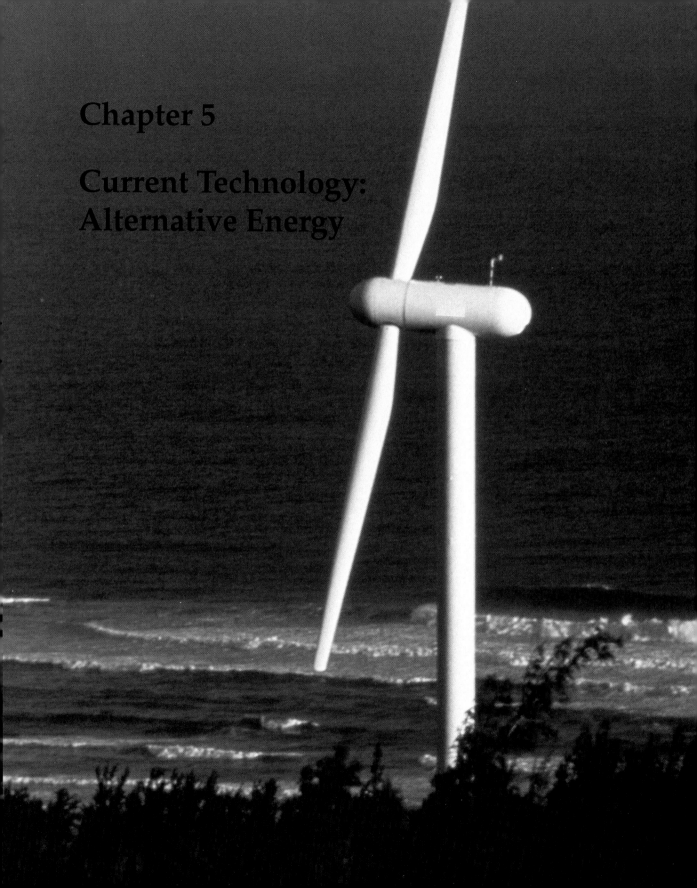

Chapter 5

Current Technology: Alternative Energy

A COUNTRY MEDICAL CLINIC in the African country of Zaire had an old diesel generator. It powered a refrigerator that stored life-saving blood, and it ran lights in the surgery. The generator required constant tinkering and lots of expensive fuel. Even so, it stopped several times, leaving nurses, doctors, and patients in the dark and ruining the blood supply. Gas and electric lines were too expensive to put in.

Recently, the diesel generator was replaced by a new power source—one that uses sunlight to create energy. It is much more reliable than the diesel. Skies in Zaire are seldom cloudy, and the clinic has more than enough energy to run the refrigerator and surgery lights.

The sun is one of many energy sources currently being tapped to help provide clean fuel. And it is a major source. There are many ways the sun's energy can be used.

Some *alternative energy* sources seem perfectly safe, others bring serious problems with them. But one thing they have in common is that their use helps us to lessen our dependence on fossil fuels.

Energy from the Sun

All life on Earth depends on the sun. Without it, nothing would grow, no rain would fall, no life would stir on Earth.

All of our power depends on the sun, too. Coal, petroleum, and natural gas were once growing things. Hydroelectric power depends on rain that falls after the sun evaporates water. The sun helps produce tides, warms ocean water, and grows biomass. These energy forms use materials that the sun has worked on. The sun's light and warmth can also be used directly for energy.

This woman from Zimbabwe displays the solar cooker she has constructed using aluminum foil. Solar cookers are helping people in developing countries reduce their dependence on wood for cooking fuel.

An Earth Experience

Building a Solar Cooker

The illustration on the next page and the instructions that follow will help you build your own solar cooker—one that you can actually use to fix yourself and your family a meal!

Find a rectangular cardboard box larger than 14 by 18 inches (36 to 46 centimeters). With adult supervision, cut out the top and most of the front (study the illustration). On another piece of cardboard, measure a circle with a radius 1 inch (2.5 centimeters) less than the height of the front opening. Locate the focal points as shown, and mark them. Cut a 1-inch-wide centered strip from the center of the circle. The half circles that remain will be the ends.

Trim another piece of cardboard $^1/_2$ inch (1.25 centimeters) shorter than the length of your box. On it, carefully start one point of an end piece and roll the curved edge along the untrimmed side. Do not let it slip. Mark where the other point ends and add $^1/_2$ inch. Cut to the length you marked.

Score (don't cut completely through) every 1 $^1/_2$ to 2 inches

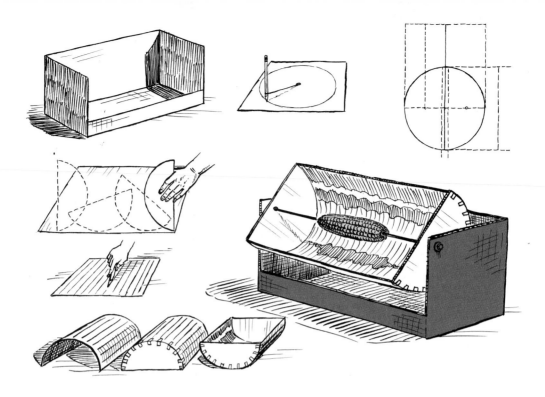

(4 to 5 centimeters) so it will bend easily. Tape the end pieces to the scored piece. Carefully glue aluminum foil with rubber cement and line the curve. This is the concentrator.

With an adult present, cut a piece of thick wire longer than your first box such as from a hanger. Hold the wire over a flame to burn off any oily coating. Push it through the focal points of the concentrator. This is the cooking rod. Connect the concentrator to the frame with bolts, nuts, and washers.

Now you're ready to cook! Choose a bright, sunny day. Start with something simple, like a hot dog or an ear of corn, strung on the cooking wire. The cooker should be aimed directly at the sun at all times. You'll probably need to adjust the cooker every half hour or so to keep it in line with the sun's rays.

The time required to cook your food will vary with the time of day and the amount of food. Your solar cooker can get very hot, so remember to use potholders. Share your results with friends!

75

Solar cells power this water pump (left) *in Africa, where other sources of energy may not be available. Solar panels on the roof* (right) *can supply much of a house's energy needs in an area where the sun shines a lot.*

Solar Cells

Sunlight has always been an attractive power source. It is nonpolluting and available to nearly everyone. Experiments with its collection and conversion into usable power began during the late 1950s. The first result was solar cells, which are also called photovoltaics (PVs).

A solar cell works because certain elements such as silicon react to sunlight by releasing some of the electrons in the atoms. That release leaves spaces in the atoms that capture electrons freed from other atoms. This movement of electrons is an electric current. Wires can pick up this current and send it to machines or storage batteries. When many solar cells are needed to get enough power, they are collected together in panels called arrays.

Solar cells are still fairly expensive, but their price has come down quite a bit in the last decade. This has been achieved by making them with new materials, as well as reducing their size. The new solar cells also work on cloudy or hazy days, whereas the original solar cells required full sunlight to function. Solar-powered calculators and watches are available. Cells are also being developed for use with home hot-water heaters, outside lights and industrial lights.

PVs are used in the United States for lighting street signs

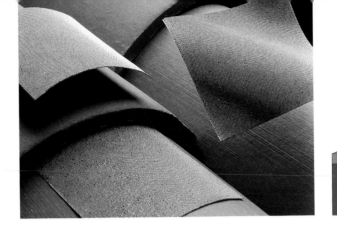

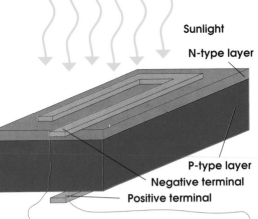

and lighthouses, and in research. India uses them to power water pumps. Japan, Germany, Italy, and Spain are hoping PV arrays can provide power for entire communities.

Collecting the Heat of the Sun

Other solar devices use the heat of the sun directly to produce steam for turning turbines. Obviously, the normal amount of sunlight hitting the Earth can't do that, otherwise lakes and rivers would boil. So these devices require mirrors to concentrate, or collect, the sunlight.

A system called solar thermal electric generation (SEG) collects sunlight in desert areas, where there is plenty of it. More than a million mirrors set on 400 acres (162 hectares) of the Mojave Desert in California move with the sun as it crosses the sky—with the help of computers. The mirrors concentrate the sun's heat on long tubes mounted above them. An oil within the tubes absorbs the sun's heat, rising to a temperature of 735 degrees F. (391 degrees C). The hot oil circulates through coils of tubing that go through water, which turns to steam for making electricity. The electricity that is created helps to fuel Los Angeles.

Because this system can work only when the sun shines, a boiler powered by natural gas provides steam when the sun is not strong enough. The owner of the system has constructed eight other systems.

Most solar cells (above) *are constructed with two layers. When sun hits the top layer of n-type silicon it releases electrons into the p-type silicon, setting up a current flow. Very thin, flexible sheets of solar cells* (left) *have been developed for easy application.*

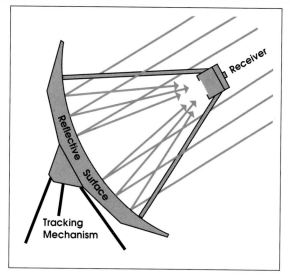

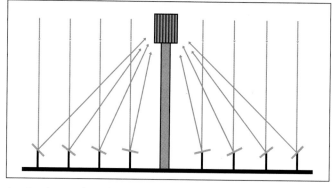

A point-focus solar collector (left) *consists of a dish-shaped reflective surface that tracks the sun through the day. It focuses the sun's rays onto a receiver, where electricity may be generated. A central receiver solar collector* (above) *uses flat mirrors on the ground, called heliostats, that track the sun and reflect its rays toward a receiver.*

Other Mirrored Collectors. Several kinds of solar collectors use mirrors. A line-focus collector has a turning mirrored surface that reflects sun onto a tube holding either water or a special heat-absorbing oil. In the water types, water is changed directly to steam for turning turbines and generators, or heating buildings. In the oil type, the heat from oil changes water to steam, which turns a turbine. Direct steam generation is more efficient but more difficult.

A point-focus collector is a mirrored dish that tracks the sun all day. The dish itself is the power-producing unit, concentrating sunlight onto a point in its center. There, water or synthetic oil is heated and used as in the line-focus collector. The point receiver itself may generate electricity.

The central receiver system consists of a collection of flat or slightly curved mirrors on the ground that turn to catch sunlight. The system reflects sunlight onto a tower-mounted receiver containing water-filled tubes. The concentrated sunlight heats the water, turning it to steam.

In a new system now being developed, heat is stored in molten salts so it can be used day or night.

Salty Energy. Solar ponds are man-made bodies of salty water. As the saltwater gets warm, it absorbs more salt, and this heated water sinks to the lower layers of the pond. The less salty, cooler, upper layers act as insulation to keep heat concentrated below. Heat can be drawn off through a coil of pipe at the bottom of the pond without disturbing the pond itself. Solar ponds can be used for both heat and power.

There are some unusual drawbacks to solar ponds. Wind can mix the salt layers together, destroying their ability to concentrate heat. Leaves and twigs that fall in the water can reduce efficiency. Salty water corrodes (eats away) metal machinery. And, if the pond leaks, groundwater could be contaminated with salt.

In Miamisburg, Ohio, a public swimming pool and a nearby recreation building were heated by a solar pond that worked successfully for several years. But there were two big problems. The first was a lack of trained maintenance workers. All debris must be cleaned out on a regular basis and the salt layers must be tested often.

The second problem was the corrosion of the heat exchanger by the salty water. The salt eats into the metal surface and eventually all the way through the heat exchanger. These parts must be replaced on a regular basis which is an expensive and time-consuming job.

Huge twin collecting ponds were built in Israel several years ago. The ponds were 269,000 square feet (25,000 square meters) and produced 2 1/2 megawatts of electricity. Eventually the heat exchanger corroded and needed to be replaced, but no one wanted to spend the money to replace it.

A working solar collection pond was built by the U.S. Bureau of Reclamation some years ago in El Paso, Texas. It is only a test facility, but it provides hot water and electricity for the Old El Paso food-processing plant.

Sorghum, a relative of corn, is a biomass crop that can be used as a renewable source of energy in the production of ethanol.

Energy from Plants and Animals: Biomass

Every day, many women and children living in developing countries gather straw and fresh cow droppings. They mix these two materials together and form patties, which they dry in the sun. The patties are used as fuel for cooking.

Straw and cow droppings are examples of biomass—any type of living matter, or by-products from living matter, that can be used for energy. Wood, peat, dried cornstalks, sawdust, grasses, organic garbage, aquatic and desert plants, even bacteria, are all biomass. Because all life depends on the sun, biomass might be considered a kind of solar energy.

Biomass is usually inexpensive, renewable, and found all over the world. However, biomass has a major disadvantage. It puts out some of the same pollutants as fossil fuels in the form of carbon dioxide, smoke, ash, and odors.

Also, in many parts of the world, trees and shrubs are being burned for heating and cooking faster than they are replaced, resulting in deforestation.

The use of such fuel doesn't sound like a very efficient

way of fueling our future. But there are new ways of turning biomass into more efficient, convenient, and clean-burning fuel products. It can be changed into gas or liquid. It can also be fermented into alcohol, which can fuel cars and trucks. One of the big advantages of the processes is that biomass can be converted from things that would otherwise be thrown away.

This scientist is researching efficient and inexpensive ways to produce ethanol from corn, especially from parts that would ordinarily have little use.

Converting Biomass. Four processes are commonly used to convert biomass into fuels. It can be heated, mixed with chemicals, compacted, or changed by microorganism digestion. Scientists are working to find new ways to coax more energy from living things.

Biomass is extremely important to developing countries that lack money to import fossil fuels. People can gather it from their fields after harvesting, cut it from forests, or collect animal wastes and trash.

Many grasses are sturdy enough to be planted on land that won't grow crops well. When the grasses are harvested, they can be pressed into pellets and used as fuel in homes or industry. Then the land is replanted. This planting and growing cycle recycles carbon—the grasses absorb carbon dioxide and give off oxygen while they grow. When they're burned, they give off carbon dioxide and consume oxygen. So the entire process does not contribute to global warming.

The biomass need not be burned directly. It can be converted into a more efficient form that can be mixed with gasoline. The two main products are alcohols, ethanol and methanol.

In many developing countries, people such as this man from Pakistan often remove crop residue from fields and use it as fuel. If this material were left to decay, it would replenish the soil.

Ethanol is usually made by processing corn or sugar cane. It has a high octane rating, which means that it can prevent knocking—the sound made by an engine when fuel ignites prematurely, before the spark. The octane rating of ethanol is 105, compared with 87 for regular gasoline and 93 for premium gasoline. In addition, fewer hydrocarbons and less carbon monoxide are produced.

Methanol is also called wood alcohol, since old production techniques required wood to make it. Now it is often made by combining carbon monoxide gas and hydrogen. It can also be produced in a variety of other ways, including the use of methane from natural gas.

Trade-Offs: Food and Fertilizer vs. Saving Oil. All this sounds good until you find out the trade-offs. Ethanol produces less energy per gallon than regular gasoline, which means that drivers must fill up more often. It is also more expensive to produce than gasoline. And when added to gasoline, it may damage car parts and help produce smog.

Since methanol can be made from natural gas, coal, wood, or garbage, its emission qualities vary greatly. As much as 10 percent less carbon dioxide is produced if methanol is made from natural gas. Almost 100 percent more is produced if it is processed from coal.

Methanol, too, produces less energy per gallon than gasoline. This fuel also makes cars difficult to start at temperatures below 50 degrees F. (10 degrees C).

Methanol and ethanol produce an emission called formaldehyde, which creates lower-atmosphere ozone, causes irritation to eyes and to respiratory systems, and is believed to cause cancer.

In poor regions of the world, the biomass used to make fuel often consists of the roots and stems left behind after harvesting a crop, along with animal droppings. Crop residues and droppings are important fertilizers that decompose and add nutrients to the soil. They also help keep rich topsoil from blowing away. Poor farmers often can't afford other fertilizers, so when crop residue and animal droppings are burned for fuel, the soil becomes poor. Smaller harvests mean more hunger.

Hungry people can't pay farmers good prices for food, either. If fuels made from grain replace gasoline, growing corn and other crops for methanol and ethanol production might pay more than raising crops for food. It's possible that many croplands would be used to grow grains for fuel instead of for food, just when the world's population is rising so rapidly and we need all the food we can grow.

Garbage Power. Did you ever think of your trash as fuel? It could be. Trash can be considered biomass, which can be burned to create energy. Of course, not everything we throw away is biomass, but much of it is. Even paper was once a tree.

An incinerator that burns 1 ton (0.9 metric ton) of garbage—including all the normal things in it such as metal, plastics, paper, and food wastes—gives off the same amount of heat energy as the burning of 1 barrel of oil.

FACT

When a crane (left) carries trash from a refuse pit to a boiler, it is one of the first steps in producing energy from waste. The burning trash heats water, creating steam that is piped off to turn turbines and generate electricity. The remaining ash is regularly cleared from the boiler to be disposed of, and the smoke is cleaned before it is released.

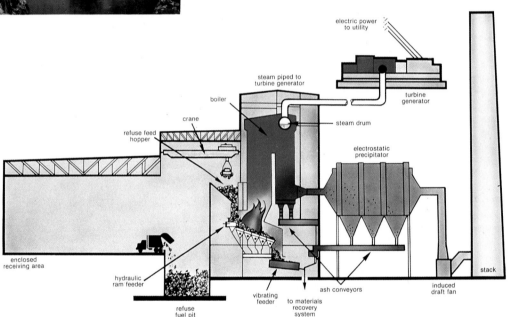

electric power
to utility

steam piped to
turbine generator

boiler

crane

refuse feed
hopper

steam drum

turbine
generator

electrostatic
precipitator

enclosed
receiving area

hydraulic
ram feeder

vibrating
feeder

to materials
recovery
system

ash conveyors

induced
draft fan

stack

refuse
fuel pit

The heat from burning waste in an incinerator can be used to boil water to run turbines. Some incinerators have oxygen jets that make the trash burn more completely, leaving little ash. Most, however, end up with unburnable stuff at the bottom where it produces dangerous toxic ash. This material, called slag, must be cleaned out and safely disposed of.

Some incinerator companies presort the trash. Newspaper, metals, plastics, Styrofoam, and glass are removed for recycling. Only paper, food wastes, yard wastes like leaves, and a few bits of plastic and metal are burned.

Tons of trash go in, electricity comes out. As you can imagine, there are several trade-offs. First, no plant can burn the trash completely. Slag or a highly toxic ash must be dealt with after combustion. Often it is dumped in landfills.

Second, trash may have an unpleasant smell, and may cause increased truck traffic and an ugly skyline so people don't want an incinerator near their homes. A nearby incinerator can cause a drop in property values. Even smokestack filters cannot keep all odor or pollution out of the air. Many people are opposed to having waste incinerators near their homes. Incinerators are a promising idea slowed by problems.

Catching the Wind

Wind energy is also a form of solar energy, since wind is produced by the unequal heating of the Earth by the sun. People have harnessed wind power since sailing ships first caught the wind to carry them through the sea.

Windmills are one of the world's oldest devices for producing mechanical power. The Arabs introduced wind power to Europe in about the twelfth century. Windmills were originally used for grinding grain into flour. They used propeller-like sails of wood and cloth to catch the wind. The sails were attached to a set of cogs that changed their vertical motion into the turning of a pole. The pole turned a large, wheel-shaped stone lying on its side on top of a similar stone. When grain was dropped between the stones, the turning pole caused them to grind together, producing flour.

The Netherlands, a country that lies mainly below sea level, is known for the many beautiful old windmills that line its shores. Starting back in the 1700s, they were used to pump water back into the sea when storms broke the dikes. Today, fossil-fueled pumps remove the seawater. However, the Dutch government plans to produce 20 percent of the country's electricity from wind by the year 2050.

Today's windmills turn mechanical energy into electrical energy, and they look very different from the old ones. Inventors and scientists have made great changes in windmills, which are now generally called wind turbines. Most have two or three blades. Modern, large wind turbines typically produce 100 to 300 kilowatts of electricity.

One type of wind turbine has an adjustable rotor, set horizontal to the ground, to which the blades are attached. This is called a horizontal-axis wind turbine (HAWT). Converters inside at the top of the tower change the movement of blades and shaft into usable electric energy. Electric cables transfer the power directly into the power system for a business or an area.

The Darrieus turbine, sometimes called an eggbeater, is a vertical-axis wind turbine or VAWT. This design has a narrow tower with two narrow blades fixed to it. Most of the

Sandia National Laboratories and the U.S. government built this enormous vertical-axis wind turbine.

machinery is at its base. This design requires a small motor to start the blades turning, but then they will turn on their own, even in winds of 15 miles (24 kilometers) per hour.

Canada, Sweden, Germany, and the United States built huge wind turbines in the 1970s. Several had 32-foot (10-meter) blades, and some were even larger. They looked good on paper, but they were unstable, developing rotor cracks and other problems. Many of the giant turbines were torn down and sold for scrap.

In 1988, the U.S. Department of Energy, the Department of Agriculture, and Sandia National Laboratories dedicated a monster with a rotor diameter of 111.5 feet (34 meters) at Bushland, Texas, in 1988. The results were not satisfactory. But sold to an electrical company, the huge VAWT still puts out 1,150 megawatts of energy per year.

Most wind turbines sold today are smaller machines that are more reliable than their huge ancestors.

Wind farms, such as this one at Altamont Pass in California made up of horizontal-axis wind turbines, take advantage of naturally windy conditions in some areas to create a clean and inexpensive source of energy.

Farming the Wind. Large-scale *wind farms* have been built in some particularly windy parts of the world to take advantage of the conditions. Some of the earliest were built in the California mountains. Heated desert air to the east rises throughout the day, pulling cool air from the ocean into the mountains. The passes—narrow gaps between mountain peaks—funnel the air, increasing its speed. At a cost of nearly $3 billion, 16,000 turbines have been built since 1981.

These wind farms contributed over 1 percent of California's total electricity in 1989. Their output is equal to that of one large nuclear plant. Comparing costs, wind turbines win—the Diablo Canyon nuclear power plant in California cost more than $5 billion.

California has 80 percent of the world's wind turbines. Denmark rates second in wind energy with 17 percent. The British government plans to build three wind farms in different parts of Great Britain. They will provide power to about 15,000 people. Britain also plans to build a wind turbine in the North Sea, where the winds are stronger than on land. Sweden is also experimenting with offshore turbines anchored to the sea floor. Canada favors the Darrieus design—which was re-invented by two Canadian scientists in the 1970s—and has wind projects in several provinces.

FACT

Wind energy costs about 7 to 9 cents per kilowatt-hour, less than the cost of nuclear power. Wind turbines replace approximately 716,400 barrels of oil yearly in the United States. About 2.8 million tons of carbon is kept out of the atmosphere by using wind-generated electricity.

Personal Wind Turbines. In the 1920s and 1930s and again in the 1970s, many farms had backyard wind machines like the one shown on page 20. Then cheap oil and electricity made most wind turbine businesses give up. They are cautiously being started again, their owners convinced that wind energy can help the environment.

A small farm in Wisconsin is a good example of the way individuals can use wind power. The farm seems normal except for the tall tower of a HAWT wind turbine on a nearby hill. It produces enough electricity to power milking machines for a small dairy herd and run lights in the barn and house. The farmer's electricity bills have dropped greatly, making his farm more efficient.

People complain about wind generators. Some think the towers are eyesores. The blades make whipping noises, which may frighten away wildlife. Bird enthusiasts grumble because many birds have been killed by wind turbines. But the trade-offs for wind power are less than those for many other sources of energy.

The Altamont, San Gorgonio, and Tehachapi passes in California have excellent conditions for using wind power. Though a wind farm such as this one takes up a lot of space, it can be constructed in an area where other things are going on. Cattle graze under these wind turbines.

Chapter 6

Ideas for the Near Future

ALL OVER THE WORLD, people and governments are currently studying and using the alternative energy sources discussed in the last chapter. But energy dreamers don't stop there. They are researching ideas that are frequently still just that—ideas. But that's where new technology comes from—people with ideas who, bit by bit, make them work.

Alternative energy systems such as solar and nuclear power currently provide only a fraction of the world's energy. Creative men and women are working to make the familiar alternative energy systems more efficient. But there are other sources that show promise for filling part of our energy requirements in the near future.

Fuel Cells

Fuel cells have the amazing ability to change the energy within a fuel directly into electric current. The idea was first developed by British physicist William Robert Grove in 1839, but practical fuel cells are still being developed.

A fuel cell is much like a car battery. However, a battery contains electrodes—positive and negative electric terminals—made of materials that react chemically and get used up. A fuel cell gets its chemicals from outside and the electrodes do not get used up, so it lasts longer.

The box of a fuel cell contains several spaces called cells. Within the cells are flat metal plates with liquid called an electrolyte circulating around them. (An electrolyte is any substance that breaks down into electrically charged atomic particles called ions when it is dissolved in a fluid.) A chemical fuel such as hydrogen is pumped into the cells, where it reacts with another gas such as oxygen that is supplied to the fuel cell from an outside source. This reaction generates an electron flow, or electricity.

In some fuel cells, the reacting substances are not pumped in but are already inside, as they are in a battery. When the cell loses energy, the chemicals can be replaced, and the cell will regain to full power.

FACT

Fuel cells were used during the United States' Apollo missions that took astronauts to the moon. They ran machinery in space where there was no means of burning regular fuels. The fuel cells used on the U.S. space shuttles produce enough power to run the equipment on board for many days.

Some electric generating stations are planning to convert part of their equipment to fuel cells in the near future. It is estimated that an array of cells the size of a tennis court could generate enough electricity to run lights and machines in a small town. Fuel cells are also being considered for electrical load-balancing. That means they will form a

Fuel cells have the ability to convert chemicals directly into electric current. Many "sandwiches" like the one shown here are clustered to make a fuel cell.

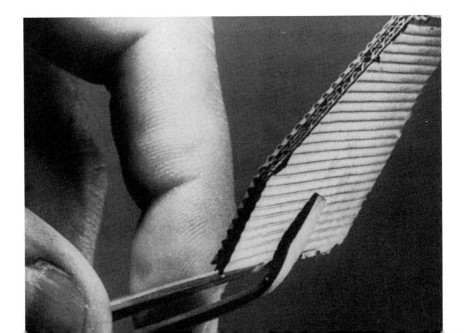

backup system, producing electricity only when the power demand is beyond the capacity of the generating station.

Research is being done to make fuel cells more efficient and to find other reactive chemicals that give more power than those already known. Perhaps part of the electricity in your house will soon come from fuel cells instead of burned coal or natural gas.

Powering an Automobile

Fuel cells are also being tested for use in powering electric cars. Most of the vehicle's power would still come from rechargeable chemical batteries. But engineers have found that when three of the batteries are replaced by three fuel cells, the electric cars have more speed and greater mileage. The cars then have a top speed of 70 miles (113 kilometers) per hour compared with about 45 or 50 miles (72 or 80 kilometers) per hour for most electric cars.

Recently a Honda CRX with fuel cells and rechargeable batteries won an electric-car race by several laps and finished with power to spare. The second-place car, which had no fuel cells, ran out of energy before the finish line.

A very large percentage of the fossil fuel we use is burned in the cylinders of cars, which emit many pollutants into the air. The search for alternative energy sources for use in cars is most important. It's unlikely that people will give up cars in the near future, so the next best thing is to give up the fossil fuel we use to run them. Fuel cells are a beginning, but other methods are also in the works.

Each year, car races are held to find the fastest car powered by electrical or solar energy. Universities and experimental laboratories from around the world participate.

Several races each year put new designs of solar cars to the test. This car, called "Sunrunner," was sponsored by a team from the University of Michigan.

Races give scientists, inventors, and engineering students the chance to prove their concepts in a challenging situation. The best of these experimental vehicles may be built by auto manufacturers in the near future.

FACT

A few inventors have converted their cars to fuels other than gasoline and natural gas. One man in Florida changed his engine to accept vegetable oil that he collected from trash bins at fast-food restaurants. The restaurant owners soon found out and put locks on their trash. The inventor was forced to buy used oil from them or pay for expensive fresh vegetable oil from a grocery. Observers reported that the car's exhaust smelled like french fries, even though it ran well. Vegetable oil is not likely to become a common fuel for cars.

Burning Hydrogen. The element hydrogen is a colorless, odorless, flammable, easily obtainable gas that has long been regarded as a potential fuel for cars. It would be an ideal fuel if inventors and scientists could solve the danger of working with it. Great care must be taken with hydrogen during storage and while filling other containers because it is explosive and can cause fires. It also costs about three times as much as gasoline.

Hydrogen-fueled cars need special equipment. As with natural gas, a pressurized tank is needed. Test cars have it mounted in the trunk. The tank feeds hydrogen to the converted engine through insulated fuel lines. Drivers of test cars seem to like the fuel. The main problems are that right now, hydrogen filling stations do not exist, and it takes a long time to fill the pressurized tank.

Recently scientists found that cooling hydrogen with liquid nitrogen, which boils at minus 320.4 degrees F. (minus 195.8 degrees C) and storing it with pellets of activated charcoal makes the gas much more stable. The charcoal acts as a sponge that holds the hydrogen until it is needed, so it's not as likely to explode.

Hydrogen fuel can be sold to the public through a converted gasoline pump after it has had time to warm up. Another method involves storing it in metal hydrides—metallic compounds of hydrogen—which makes it safe. It is separated when it is pumped into the car. These methods make hydrogen a potential replacement for fossil fuels.

The pressurized fuel tank for a hydrogen test car is mounted in the trunk.

New Engines. The cylinders in a standard car engine go through four strokes in a cycle: the fuel enters, it's compressed, the spark plug ignites it, and the exhaust gases are released.

In 1974, Ralph Sarich of Perth, Australia, designed a car engine that works with only two strokes. It has fewer moving parts, is half the weight and half the size, and produces 30 percent more power than a regular four-stroke engine. The two-stroke engine also puts out 95 percent less carbon monoxide emissions.

The only drawback is that high oxygen levels in the exhaust make it impossible to reduce smog-producing chemicals with a standard catalytic converter. That part of the system will have to be redesigned for the new engine.

Ford Motor Company, General Motors, and Subaru have purchased licenses and plan to build two-stroke automobile, aircraft, motorcycle, and power-boat engines. Fuji Heavy Industries and Toyota Motor Company in Japan are developing their own two-strokes. This engine may revolutionize the automobile industry and at the same time help save Earth's atmosphere.

FACT

João Gurgel of Brazil has developed a small, two-cylinder car that gets up to 80 miles (129 kilometers) per hour and costs about half the price of a small car in the United States. The engine operation of Gurgel's BR-800 is controlled by an electronic computerized ignition system.

Using The Heat Within the Earth

As you read in Chapter 4, there are already ways to use the heat within the Earth as an energy source. The people who are thinking far into the future, however, have dreamed up other possibilities.

Geo-pressure System

To Generator

Top Soil Layer

Rock Layer

Pressurized Heated Liquid

Geo-Pressure Systems. Closed pockets of hot water, sometimes hot water mixed with methane, lie deep under the Earth's surface. Because of compression and the Earth's interior heat, the liquid heats up and expands. The expansion makes the fluid's pressure increase. It's possible to drill down to such pockets, tap this heated and pressurized water, and cap it off, much like an oil well. The fluid could then be used to drive turbines.

Geo-pressure systems are still in the theory stage. There are some drawbacks that will cause developers to hesitate before drilling. Geologists know that when pressurized water is removed from the Earth, soil and rock can collapse above it. Such a collapse is called a sink, or land subsidence. Sinks can occur without warning, creating danger for people, animals, and structures. Geo-pressure systems may be more environmentally hazardous than energy needs demand. Engineers and scientists continue to work on them.

Hot Dry Rock. Another proposed geothermal energy concept is known as hot dry rock. Everywhere on the planet, hard rock under the Earth's surface is heated to high temperatures by the natural decay of nearby radioactive minerals. Engineers hope to tap into this heat source by drilling vertical holes into the rocks and injecting pressurized water. Other holes allow the water to be pumped back to the surface. It could be heated just enough to run the water through pipes to nearby businesses or communities for home heating and industrial needs. Or it could be allowed to heat enough to turn to steam, which would turn turbines.

Growing Our Fuel

Biomass is already in use as a source of energy, but it has the potential to play an even more important role in filling the world's needs. It's estimated that about 7 to 10 percent of the current energy demand could be supplied by biomass.

The advantage of using biomass is that it can be converted into fuels, such as ethanol and methanol, which can be substituted for fossil fuels.

The best sources of biomass currently are trees and grasses. Scientists are trying to develop strains of these plants that will grow quickly and use less water and fertilizer than normal crops.

Additional research is looking into other sources of biomass.

Oily Plants. Imagine a field of poinsettia plants as far as you can see. But these red-flowered plants are not grown for Christmas decoration. They are grown for oil! The milky liquid within these plants can be refined and used to replace petroleum. Other oily plants produce oils in seeds or fruits. Rubber plants produce a similar substance. The scrubby creosote bush from the southwestern United States and Mexico is being investigated as a living oil well. These are only a few of the oily plants available for study.

Growing plants for oil is still very experimental. Other alternative energy sources are much more promising. However, the possibilities of growing oily plants deserve discussion and further experimentation.

One of the drawbacks to growing fuel-producing plants is that thousands of acres are necessary to produce a profitable crop. It would take millions of plants to obtain enough oil to fill a fraction of our fuel needs. But genetic engineers may be able to change the genes within the cells of the plants slightly so that they produce more oil naturally.

Algae Fuel. Green scummy stuff in the gas tank? Why not? Scientists at the Solar Energy Research Institute, or SERI, in Golden, Colorado, are working with simple water plants called algae. They are trying to make them produce more lipids, such as fats and oil. Lipids are hydrocarbons, the same burnable stuff found in fossil fuels.

Growing algae in salt water, scientists carefully feed it nitrogen and other trace elements. They make sure that sunlight hits the plants at least half the growing time. This combination has produced excellent results. After harvesting, algae is heated with a mixture of hydrochloric acid and methanol. The result is diesel oil, which can be further refined into gasoline.

Algae are ideal for this purpose because they grow well in nearly any damp area. Scientists estimate that a pond about 70 feet (21 meters) in diameter, fitted with a machine that spreads carbon dioxide bubbles throughout the water, can produce 794 gallons (3,005 liters) of fuel every year. They hope algae can eventually yield 8 percent of the United States' diesel and gasoline needs by 2010.

Such fuel produces carbon dioxide when it burns, but the CO_2 would be reabsorbed if the plants burned were replaced by new growth.

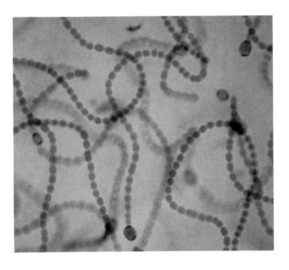

People may someday grow large crops of algae and use them to produce oil to power our cars and trucks.

More Experimental Generation of Electricity

Other methods of producing power for people are being investigated at laboratories around the world. Some of them are quite complex and futuristic.

MHD. One concept that scientists are trying to make practical is magnetohydrodynamics (MHD). MHD is already being used to produce small amounts of power, but it has not yet generated the amount of power that scientists originally expected.

A *magneto* is a small generator with one or more magnets surrounded by a magnetic field. *Hydrodynamics* is the study of the motion and action of fluids. An MHD power generator uses the interaction of fluids that conduct electricity and a magnetic field. The fluid used may be a liquid metal or an ionized (electrically charged) gas. Either one of these can be passed through the magnetic field. As it travels, the metal or gas produces electricity that can be picked up directly by electrodes within the magnetic field.

Scientists have been working on MHD for more than a hundred years, starting with British chemist Sir Humphry Davy. Some industries are already using MHD for small power needs. Scientists are working to improve its output. John Nuckolls, former director of physics at the Lawrence Livermore National Laboratory, believes that MHD can be combined with nuclear fusion (see the next chapter) to bring energy from that source closer to reality.

Another Not-Quite. Electrogasdynamics (EGD) is another concept that has not produced as much energy as originally hoped. It passes a stream of gas that is full of electrically

This 180-ton (162-metric ton) superconducting magnet is one of the world's largest. It was built for energy research by Argonne National Laboratory in Illinois.

charged atomic particles through an electrical field. The field works against the motion of the particles, slowing them down. The result is an increasing electrical direct current that can be run through wires to wherever power is needed.

Like MHD, EGD could be used for small-need power production in several industries. Scientists are still working on enlarging the capacity of the process to produce electricity more efficiently.

Many researchers are working on ways to replace fossil fuels, so that our world is free of the pollution they cause. Some of the concepts discussed here are likely to become practical within the next decade or so. Others have been researched for many years and may still have many more years to go. The important thing is that scientists continue researching ways to save our planet from the devastating effects of fossil-fuel use.

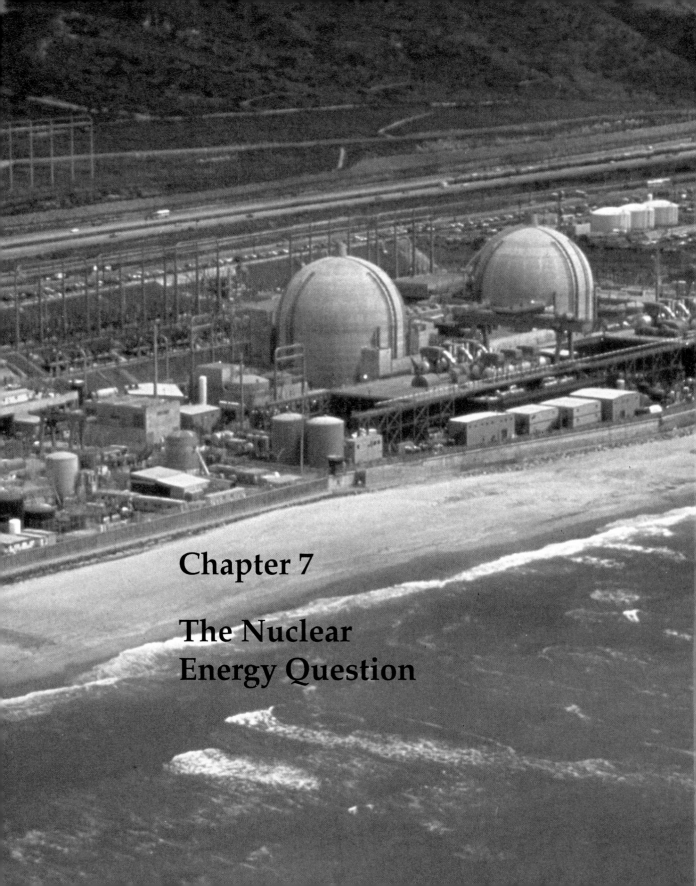

Chapter 7

The Nuclear
Energy Question

PROBABLY THE MOST CONTROVERSIAL of all alternative energy sources is nuclear power. People in favor of it say it is a relatively cheap and clean way to provide energy for our world, without ever having to run out. But those opposed to nuclear power say that it is extremely dangerous. Though many things are done to try to keep nuclear power plants safe, there have been a few accidents around the world, one of which took many lives.

Before you decide how you feel about nuclear power, you should understand how this energy source works.

Radioactivity. Certain types of matter give off energy without any outside help. This energy is called radioactivity. It is caused by the transformation of one type of atom into another, lighter atom by neutrons, protons and electrons leaving. It was first discovered in the element uranium, which eventually decays into lead. Radioactivity has since been found elsewhere. It is a natural but dangerous process.

Normally, there's not enough radioactivity going on to harm people. It's only when a large amount of decaying atomic matter is gathered in one place that the harmful effects may become significant.

Exposure to too much radioactivity can cause burns, sickness, and even death. Moderate amounts can cause birth defects and health problems in the elderly. Exposure is known to cause cancers. But if carefully and properly managed, radioactivity is a potentially valuable source of energy.

A special type of radioactivity involves the disintegration of atoms and is called *nuclear fission,* meaning "splitting." The nuclear fission process was first controlled by humans in a device built under the stadium at Stagg Field at the University of Chicago in December 1942 under the leadership of Nobel Prize winner Dr. Enrico Fermi. The knowledge gained in the process was used in the development of the atomic bombs, which were dropped on Japan to end World War II. But the process is beneficial in nuclear power plants.

Nuclear Decay to Energy. Neutrons are a tiny part of the nucleus of an atom. Unlike protons and electrons, they have no electrical charge. Neutrons and protons bond together in different numbers in the nucleus of atoms to form the different chemical elements.

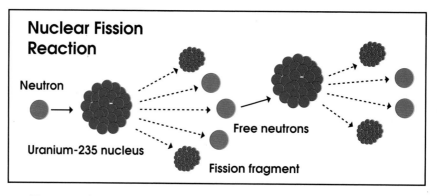

During the process of splitting atoms, a nucleus of a uranium atom gains a neutron. The nucleus then splits, releasing energy and several neutrons. These neutrons can hit other nuclei, which break apart, releasing more neutrons, which hit others, and so on. A chain reaction has been started. If the chain reaction can be controlled, the energy given off can be set to work.

There are several types of nuclear power plants. The main one in actual use is the light-water reactor. There are a few breeder reactors being used, mainly in research.

A nuclear research facility in San Diego, California, investigates ways to produce nuclear energy for the future more safely.

The Light-Water Reactor. In a light-water reactor, the chain reaction is controlled in an atomic assembly, also called an atomic pile. This is a series of hollow zirconium-alloy rods packed with tiny pellets of uranium dioxide. These fuel rods are fastened together as the reactor core.

Water in pipes coiled around the core is heated until it turns to steam. The steam exits by another pipe and turns a turbine, which is connected to a generator. Electricity flows out to the energy grid through wires. The steam condenses to hot water, which is sometimes released into a lake, river, or bay to cool.

Nuclear power plants need a large containment structure—a building of layered concrete and steel many feet thick—over the atomic assembly to guard against the danger of explosion or radiation leak. Because of the dangerous radiation, work inside the assembly is controlled by computers and robots that are managed by people located in a secure area far from the reactor core.

FACT

Nuclear energy fills about 10 percent of the world's electricity needs. European countries such as France and Germany have continued to build light-water reactors. Some of the Soviet republics, Great Britain, and Japan have also continued to build these reactors as electrical power sources. No new light-water reactors have been built in the United States since the late 1970s.

Breeder Reactors. Breeder reactors use the element thorium for fuel, or a type of uranium that is much less radioactive than the uranium used in light-water reactors. When neutrons strike the fuel atoms, the fuel is changed into a different, more reactive material, such as plutonium, by gaining neutrons. The neutrons are slowed during the process so they will hit more atoms and release more energy.

Each breeder reactor can make fuel for itself and three light-water reactors. Such a reactor is much more efficient, too. A light-water reactor uses less than 1 percent of its fuel, but a breeder reactor uses 70 percent.

There has never been a working breeder reactor in the United States. One was designed and almost completed at Clinch River, Tennessee, but the project was abandoned for several reasons. First, many people feared that an accident would release nuclear radiation from the containment chamber. Second, there were many costly problems with the construction. And third, some people feared that even strict security could not stop terrorists determined to steal plutonium to make nuclear weapons.

Though several breeder reactors have been constructed for research by laboratories and universities, no commercial

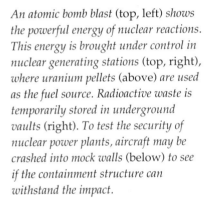

An atomic bomb blast (top, left) shows the powerful energy of nuclear reactions. This energy is brought under control in nuclear generating stations (top, right), where uranium pellets (above) are used as the fuel source. Radioactive waste is temporarily stored in underground vaults (right). To test the security of nuclear power plants, aircraft may be crashed into mock walls (below) to see if the containment structure can withstand the impact.

These scientists are conducting tests on the fuel rods of a light-water nuclear reactor, to see how the rods would perform in case of an accident. When the fuel contained in the rods is worn out, it becomes nuclear waste, which is a major environmental problem.

breeder reactors are planned by the U.S. government.

However, breeder reactors have been built in other countries. Some of these are test models, constructed to see how well they work. Great Britain has a breeder reactor, and France, impressed by their efficiency, has several. More are in the planning or construction phases in Germany, Japan, India, and Italy.

Nuclear Safety. Printing out the requirements for containing nuclear radiation at a generating plant takes many thick books. Not many reactors were built without containment structures, and most of those were very early experimental models. The containment structure is intended to stop radiation in case of a leak.

An accident at Chernobyl, near Kiev in the Soviet Union, in 1986 released a cloud of radiation. The reactor was an older type without a full containment structure. During an experiment by technicians, one of four reactors exploded and caught fire. About one-quarter of the plant's radioactivity was released in steam. Two people died in the blast, 21 died shortly thereafter from radiation exposure, and hundreds, even thousands, of others will probably die of radiation-caused cancer. More than 135,000 people were evacuated from the area. High levels of radiation were found as far away as Scandinavia and Switzerland. Milk and crops all over Europe had to be destroyed. The memory still gives some people nightmares.

Nuclear power-plant designers are developing fission reactors which, they claim, cannot explode or release radiation. These designs probably won't be built for at least ten years, but it is hoped that they will help people trust nuclear reactors as safe power sources.

The Problem with Used Fuel. Besides the threat of radiation leakage, spent (used) fuel is a big problem. Every year, one-quarter to one-third of each reactor's fuel has to be replaced. The old fuel is carefully transferred by robotic machines into a pool of water, where it remains for many years until much—but not all—of its radioactivity is lost.

In Europe, Japan, the Soviet republics, and India, spent fuel from reactors is taken to a reprocessing plant. There the old fuel is purified. The tiny radioactive pellets are repacked with new fuel into hollow rods and fastened into the core.

The U.S. government decided to have no commercial reprocessing done in the United States. Currently, all U.S. spent fuel is sitting in temporary storage waiting for a decision to be made on how to store it permanently.

The nuclear waste left behind after energy is produced is still highly radioactive. Scientists hope to someday develop a foolproof way to store or destroy it. In the meantime, nuclear waste is often stored in huge, underground facilities. These containers will be covered with soil.

A radioactive-waste site below Carlsbad, New Mexico, is ready for use. Radioactive material would be carefully sealed in containers that do not rust or wear away by chemical action. The canisters would be stored in 56 rooms—each as large as a football field—cut out from a salt formation 2,140 feet (653 meters) below the desert.

The facility is called the Waste Isolation Pilot Plant (WIPP). The U.S. government intends it to be primarily for waste generated from the manufacture of nuclear weapons. The facility was to have opened for testing in 1988, but technical problems and lawsuits have delayed the opening.

When the U.S. Department of Energy announced a six-year test, the state of New Mexico filed suit against it. The basis of the suit is a disagreement over how much nuclear waste should be stored and closely observed during the test. The DOE wants to fill 1 percent of the facility, while the state officials want only half that amount. They fear that the waste would not be removed if the WIPP does not pass the test.

The construction of a huge underground facility at Yucca Mountain, Nevada, was proposed for the storage of nuclear waste from light-water reactors. Environmental questions, such as how water moves through the rock chambers where the radioactive containers would be stored and the possibilities of earthquakes, have not been answered.

A major problem associated with a nuclear waste storage site is that of security for the next 10,000 years. That is the half-life (the time it takes for half of the material to lose its radioactivity) of some components of radioactive fuel.

Nuclear: Yes or No? Years of research and billions of dollars have been spent on building the nuclear plants currently in use. One of the last built in the United States was at Diablo Canyon, California. It cost more than $5 billion. Public fear of radioactivity, spent-fuel storage problems, and the high costs of building and licensing the reactors—the trade-offs—have almost halted construction of nuclear reactors in the United States. Other nations have decided to build new reactors and are increasing the percentage of energy they get from this source. But many of those countries are also reconsidering their commitment to nuclear power.

What do you think? Does our need to stop burning the fossil fuels that endanger our planet win out over the threat of radiation?

Nuclear Fusion

Nuclear fusion is the type of tremendous energy that occurs in the stars. It has been known here on Earth in powerful fusion bombs. Scientists all over the world have been working since the early 1950s to harness this reaction for useful purposes. If the problems are solved, energy from nuclear fusion could replace fossil fuels. But that is a big "if." Many experts doubt that fusion will ever work well enough to be a practical source of energy.

Fusion is different from fission. Fission is the splitting of naturally radioactive atomic particles to release energy. Fission is the energy that has been used for the last thirty years in nuclear power plants. Fusion jams nonradioactive atomic particles together for the same result.

An easy way to remember the difference is by looking at

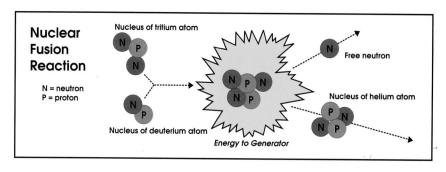

Nuclear Fusion Reaction

N = neutron
P = proton

Nucleus of tritium atom

Nucleus of deuterium atom

Energy to Generator

Free neutron

Nucleus of helium atom

the periodic table of elements in an encyclopedia or chemistry book. Very light elements—mainly hydrogen and helium—can be used for fusion. Very heavy elements, such as uranium and plutonium, can be fissioned to produce energy.

There are many problems to overcome in producing fusion power. One of the most difficult is that atomic particles tend to fly away from one another instead of readily joining. This repulsion is solved by heating fuel to high temperatures. However, this means that a lot of energy from other sources must be poured in before any comes out. Scientists are working toward breakeven, when energy put in and energy coming from fusion will be equal. Once started, fusion can be continually sustained. Its primary fuel, deuterium—a form of hydrogen—is found in water.

The devices in which the reaction occurs are often called thermonuclear reactors. They require the use of a special form of matter called plasma. Plasma, instead of being made up of whole atoms like regular matter, consists of loose nuclei, ions, protons, and electrons. It can be created by heating certain gases such as deuterium to such a high temperature that the atoms fall apart. When these parts come together again to form whole atoms, energy is given off. The big problem is how to keep the plasma in one place so that these reactions can occur.

Fusion Reactors. There are currently two types of prototype machines that are considered promising.

The tokamak uses huge magnets to confine the plasma in the shape of a doughnut. Urged into motion by an electrical force, the plasma circles inside the chamber.

At this point, scientists hope to cause a chain reaction that will make fusion a self-sustaining energy source. When this is accomplished, energy from a tokamak will be used to heat a cooling liquid like water, which will produce steam to turn turbines and make electricity.

The stellarator, the second prototype machine, is similar but doesn't need an electric transformer to produce electric currents in its plasma. Tubes that fire hot plasma to encourage the fusion process are spaced around the outside. The additional plasma heats the fuel, increasing the reaction until there is enough energy given off to generate electric power.

No one knows just what the future of nuclear fusion may be. If it does become an energy source someday, the cost of fuel will be lower than that of coal. Unfortunately, breakeven is still years away, and practical fusion energy plants are more years behind that.

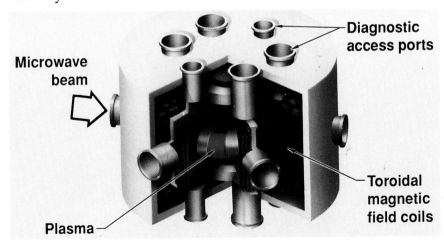

The tokamak, one promising form of nuclear fusion reactor, uses plasma circling inside a chamber to produce a fusion reaction. The tokamak was first built at the Kurchatov Institute in Moscow in 1970.

Chapter 8

Taking Action

BY THE YEAR 2030 YOU MAY BE rubbing elbows with 10 billion people. Weather could be a few degrees warmer. Washington, DC, along with many other coastal cities worldwide, could be facing serious floods. The brownish haze of pollution that we now see only occasionally could hang in the skies all the time.

But the likelihood of these problems occurring could be greatly reduced if we take control of fossil-fuel pollution now. That means governments, industries, and ourselves as individuals all need to work at changing habits for the problem to be solved.

What can you do?

Fuel-Efficient Purchases

Motors that work more efficiently is one reason world energy needs have not risen as much as expected in the last 20 years. Appliance manufacturers particularly have been working to make their equipment use fuel more efficiently. But you need to do your part by buying wisely.

When your parents replace an old appliance, have them check labels on the new one carefully. Getting a high-efficiency refrigerator, freezer, or air conditioner might cost a little more, but it will save money and energy over time. Many older refrigerator-freezers consume twice as much energy as some of the best new ones on the market. Also, fancier equipment uses more energy. For example, a refrigerator that hands you ice cubes through the door uses a great deal more energy than one that you must open.

Special tags on certain appliances show their SEER numbers. SEER stands for Seasonal Energy Efficiency Rating. It is a percentage that rates the overall energy efficiency of an appliance such as a furnace or air conditioner.

Discuss the SEER ratings with your parents before they buy an appliance. High SEERs are worth looking for. The appliance may cost a little more, but the cost is usually paid back in energy savings over a period of months or years. And you will be helping the Earth by cutting down on fossil-fuel usage.

The same goes for buying a car. Choose carefully. Compare several models. Get the highest mileage per gallon possible in a style that fits your needs. After you or your parents get a new car, keep it in good repair. Have the air conditioning checked on a regular basis. Otherwise, it could be leaking chlorofluorocarbons (CFCs) into the air. These chemicals are endangering the ozone layer far above the Earth that protects us from ultraviolet rays of the sun. Think about not having an air conditioner in your car.

Living Lightly

Use a bicycle or mass transit whenever possible. Carpooling to school, work, and social events is another good way to save energy.

Don't leave the television talking to itself. Make sure that air conditioning or heating is not on when the windows are open. Are there rubber sweeps on the bottoms of your outside doors at home? How about draft

If you use public transportation instead of taking a car where you need to go, you will use far less fuel and create much less pollution. If there is no mass transit near your home, consider walking or riding your bike.

stoppers, those tubes of sand or other material put at the inside base of an outside door? Both of these simple devices keep cold air out and warm air in.

Ask your parents to have an energy audit done on your house. Just call your local electric company. For a small charge they will send someone to look over your house and offer suggestions on saving energy. These might be little things like putting up a thick curtain over a glass door or pulling the blinds on south-facing windows in the summer. Some suggestions might call for more extensive changes, such as insulating the attic or buying a new door.

Finding Drafts in Your House

You can check for drafts around windows and doors yourself. With adult supervision, light a candle and hold the flame a few inches from a window. Move the candle all around the frame. Does the flame flicker? If the flame dances, you've got a draft coming in through the window frame. Check each window and each outside door in your house. You can easily fix most frame leaks around windows and doors with caulk.

Lights. What kind of light bulbs does your family use? Fluorescent bulbs give the most light for the least electricity. A compact, screw-in fluorescent bulb will last ten times longer than a traditional incandescent, and it is four times as efficient. They cost more to buy, but they cost much less to run. Also, try to use fewer bulbs with higher wattage. When considering energy usage, one is better than two. Be sure to turn off lights when you leave a room.

FACT

It's estimated that if everyone in the United States were to convert to the energy-efficient, economical lighting sources available today, as many as 40 large, fossil-fuel-burning power plants could be shut down.

Planting Trees. Plants gave us fossil fuels, and we can use plants to help conserve them. A few trees around your house could help reduce summer energy use by up to 50 percent. If your parents own your house, ask them for help in planning where trees could go. The south and west sides of the house are best. You might want to check with a local nursery about the kinds of trees that will grow well in your region.

If you live in a rented house or in an apartment, perhaps you know someone in the country who will let you plant a tree there. Remember, just one tree takes from 25 to 45 pounds (11 to 20 kilograms) of carbon out of the air every year. That helps the global warming problem.

Recycle. Recycling the packaging from items you use regularly can be an important way of conserving energy, since it usually takes less energy to recycle something than it does to produce it from raw materials. With a little organization, you can keep paper, metals, plastic, cardboard, and glass out of landfills. If you're not in an area that recycles with the regular weekly trash pickup, check and see if there's a recycling center nearby. You can store recyclables in your basement, garage, or shed and take them into the center once a month.

Recycling aluminum uses 95 percent less energy than producing aluminum products from raw materials. Recycling paper uses 60 percent less energy than manufacturing paper from virgin timber. And recycling a glass jar saves enough energy to light a 100-watt light bulb for four hours.

Does your school recycle? If not, help set up a club with one of your teachers as coordinator. Recycle paper from the office and classroom work, metal from the cafeteria kitchen, and cans from the soda machine. Collect them in bins or sacks and take them to the recycling center.

Keeping Tabs on the Government

Find out if your congressional or provincial representatives are serious about environmental issues. Discuss these people and their views with your parents. Watch television news and read the papers to find out how they vote on important issues. If the office is local, call and ask how your representative stands on such matters as reduction in fossil-fuel use and nuclear-waste storage. Perhaps you could invite a politician to your school to speak, or get involved in a re-election campaign.

It takes much less energy to recycle paper and other products than it does to create them from raw materials. Collect everything that can be recycled from your trash and turn it in to a recycler.

Writing Letters. In writing a letter in which you express your opinion on controversial issues, follow these tips:

1. Make your letter one page or less. Cover only one subject in each letter.

2. Introduce yourself and tell why you, personally, are for or against the issue.

3. Be clear and to the point.

4. Be specific on whether you want the person to vote "yes" or "no."

5. Write as an individual. The environmental groups you belong to will have already let the legislator know their stand on the issue.

6. When you get a response, write a follow-up letter to re-emphasize your position and give your reaction to your legislator's comments.

On issues concerning state legislation or to express your opinion about actions taken by your state or provincial environmental or natural resources agency, you can write to:

Your local state or provincial legislator. Check your local library to discover his or her name.

The governor of your state or premier of your province. Write in care of your state or provincial capital.

The director of your state or province's department of natural resources or related environmental agency. Check your local library for the specific person and the address.

On issues concerning federal legislation or to express your opinion about actions taken by the federal government, you can write to:

Your state's two U.S. senators. Check at your local library to discover their names.

The Honorable _____
U.S. Senate
Washington, DC 20510

Your local congressman. Check at your local library to discover his or her name.

The Honorable _____
U.S. House of Representatives
Washington, DC 20515

Your local provincial or federal member of Parliament. Check at your local library to discover his or her name.

> The Honorable _____
> House of Commons
> Ottawa, Ontario, Canada K1A 0A6

The President of the United States. He has the power to veto, or turn down, bills approved by the Senate and the House of Representatives as well as to introduce bills of his own. He also has final control over what the U.S. Department of Energy and other agencies do.

> President _____
> The White House
> 1600 Pennsylvania Avenue, NW
> Washington, DC 20501

The Prime Minister of Canada.

> The Honorable _____
> House of Commons
> Ottawa, Ontario, Canada K1A 0A6

Join Organizations

There are many groups of people who care about protecting the planet from pollution. They check on what is happening around the world to make sure that places that need help get it. They also do their best to inform the general public about such things, knowing that an aroused public often can do things that individuals cannot. Many of them have local chapters that welcome all the help they can get.

The following organizations are among those that play a major role in fighting for energy efficiency:

American Council for an Energy Efficient Economy, Suite 535, 1001 Connecticut Ave., NW, Washington, DC 20036

Canadian Wildlife Federation, 1673 Carling Ave., Ottawa, Ontario, Canada K2A 3Z1

Center for Environmental Information, 99 Court St., Rochester, NY 14604

Energy Conservation Coalition, 1525 New Hampshire Ave., NW, Washington, DC 20036

Environmental Action, 1525 New Hampshire Ave., NW, Washington, DC 20036

Environmental Defense Fund, 1616 P St., NW, Washington, DC 20036

National Audubon Society, 950 Third Ave., New York, NY 10022

National Energy Foundation, 5160 Wiley Post Way, Suite 200, Salt Lake City, UT 84116

National Wildlife Federation, 1400 16th St., NW, Washington, DC 20036

Natural Resources Defense Council, 1350 New York Avenue, NW, #300, Washington, DC 20005

Sierra Club, 730 Polk St., San Francisco, CA 94109

Union of Concerned Scientists, 26 Church St., Cambridge MA 02238

Wilderness Society, 1400 I St., NW, 10th Floor, Washington, DC 20005

Worldwatch Institute, 1776 Massachusetts Ave., NW, Washington, DC 20036

Everyone needs to be involved in saving energy, both to conserve fossil fuels and to prevent them from damaging our planet further. Developing new fuels and cleaning up the Earth are big jobs. But that does not mean they can't be done. With work and determination, we can change our fuel-wasting habits and encourage others to do so, too. Our dependence on fossil fuels must be changed, and soon. After all, Earth is the only home we have. We must all dedicate time and effort to save it.

GLOSSARY

biomass – any growing thing, or by-product of growing things, that can be burned or fermented to produce energy.

chlorofluorocarbons (CFCs) – These are complex chemicals that contain carbon and chlorine. CFCs play a part in global warming by trapping heat in the lower atmosphere. But they also rise into the upper atmosphere where they damage the protective ozone layer. Freon used in air conditioners is a common type of CFC.

coke – coal heated to burn out impurities, such as trapped gases. When used as fuel it burns much cleaner than regular coal.

electrode – a material, usually a metal, through which electric current enters or exits electrical equipment. Electrons move from the anode (the positive electrode) to the cathode (the negative electrode).

electrolyte – any chemical through which an electric current will flow when the chemical is dissolved in water.

electron – a negatively charged particle that moves around the nucleus of an atom. Electricity consists of the flow of electrons through wire.

emissions – particles or gases released during the burning of chemicals or fossil fuels.

ethanol – an alcohol made from fermented biomass. It is used to replace gasoline.

fossil fuels – natural gas, coal, and oil. The most commonly used fuels, they were formed over millions of years by compression and heating of partially decomposed organic matter.

generator – a device that produces electricity by changing mechanical energy (the energy of motion) into electrical energy. The motion of a coil of copper wire within a magnetic field produces electron flow within the wire.

geothermal energy – heat stored in the Earth, often in water or rocks. This heat can be used for energy production.

global warming – the gradual increase in the temperature of the Earth above the level it is normally kept at by the greenhouse effect. It is caused by the addition of carbon dioxide and other gases to the atmosphere, primarily from burning fossil fuels.

greenhouse effect – the trapping of the sun's heat within the atmosphere by certain naturally occurring gases such as water vapor and carbon dioxide, causing Earth's temperature to stay warmer than it would otherwise be.

half-life – the time required for disintegration of half the atoms in a radioactive substance. It determines how long spent fuel from nuclear reactors would have to be stored away from living things.

hydroelectric power – the production of electric power by using the force of falling water to turn turbines.

methane (CH_4) – the major component of natural gas. Also a greenhouse gas, it is released during combustion of coal and wood.

methanol – a poisonous alcohol made from fermented wood, coal, garbage, or gas that is used as a substitute for gasoline.

neutron – a particle in the nucleus of an atom that has no charge.

nitrous oxide (N_2O) – a chemical compound released into the air from fertilizers and burning wood. It is a greenhouse gas.

nuclear fission – the splitting apart of the nuclei of atoms during which part of the mass is changed into energy. This energy has been used in tremendously destructive weapons as well as to generate electricity.

nuclear fusion – the joining of the nuclei of atoms, usually of heavy hydrogen or tritium. This forms a nucleus with more mass, such as helium. The process, which gives off energy, also takes place in the sun and in hydrogen bombs. Scientists hope to harness it and make a sustainable energy source.

nucleus – the central part of the atom, made up of protons and neutrons. In a neutral atom the charges of the protons are balanced by the negatively charged electrons.

ozone (O_3) – a molecule made up of three atoms of oxygen. It is formed when sunlight acts on oxygen. In the lower atmosphere, it is a harmful part of smog. In the stratosphere, ozone helps prevent sunlight's damaging ultraviolet rays from reaching Earth.

peak load – the times of heaviest use of electrical utilities, often during summer heat when air conditioners are used.

photovoltaics (PVs) – devices that are capable of producing electricity directly from the action of sunlight on silicon and other materials. They are important as a clean source of energy. Also called solar cells.

proton – a particle in the nucleus of an atom that has a positive electric charge.

smog – urban air pollution made of smoke and various gases.

solar cells – see photovoltaics.

stratosphere – the region of Earth's atmosphere above the level where weather is formed. The ozone layer lies within it.

sulfur dioxide (SO_2) – a pollutant caused by combustion of sulfur-containing fuels like coal. It contributes to acid rain.

turbine – a device, consisting of a series of blades, that turns a shaft which in turn causes the coil in a generator to rotate. The turbine is caused to turn by the force of steam, water, or wind hitting the blades. Large quantities of fossil fuels are burned to create steam for the production of electricity.

INDEX

Bold number = illustration

PHOTO SOURCES

The Acid Rain Foundation, Inc.: 35 (right)
American Academy of Science: 95
American Coal Foundation: 12, 31
American Electric Power: 50
Courtesy of the American Petroleum Institute: 13, 21, 24, 28, 30, 36, 53, 59 (bottom right), 81
Argonne National Laboratory: 92, 101
Arizona Department of Commerce: 76 (right)
Atlantic Richfield Co.: 40 (right)
Steve Ausmus: 52, 70
Jean Blashfield: 86
Chevron Corporation: 40 (left)
Ralph Clark: 45 (top)
Conoco, Inc.: 16 (left)
S.C. Delaney/EPA: 6, 11 (bottom)
Courtesy of the Energy Office of the Arizona Department of Commerce: 75
General Motors: 49, 94
Gulf Oil Corporation: 16 (right), 105
Hawaiian Electric Renewable Systems, Inc.: 72
Hydro-Quebec: 61
Icelandair: 68
Industry, Science and Technology, Canada, Photo: 38, 114, 116
Institute for Local Self Reliance: 54
William Keller: 8
Courtesy of Lawrence Livermore National Laboratory: 113
Beth Mittermaier: 2
National Aeronautics and Space Administration: 90
National Energy Laboratory of Hawaii Authority: 65, 66 (both), 99
National Park Service: 59 (bottom left)
National Solid Wastes Management Association: 119
Courtesy of the New York Power Authority: 60 (both)
Occidental Oil Corporation: 14
Photocomm, Grass Valley, California: 76 (left)
Quaker State Oil Refining Corp.: 22
Shell Oil Company: 17
Solar Box Cookers International: 74
Solar Energy Research Institute: 41
Southern California Edison Company: 9, 59 (top), 102, 107 (top right)
Standard Oil Company of California: 18
United States Bureau of Reclamation photo by V. Jetley: 62
United States Coast Guard: 37
Courtesy of the United States Council for Energy Awareness: 107 (center left)
United States Department of Agriculture Forest Service, Pacific Northwest Region: 11 (top)
United States Department of Agriculture Soil Conservation Service: 29
United States Department of Energy: 80, 87 (both), 108, 107 (top left, center right, bottom both), 110
United States Library of Congress: 25
United States Windpower, Inc., Livermore, California: 89
Wheelabrator Environmental Systems, Inc.: 84 (both)
Peter Wiebe, Woods Hole Oceanographic Institute: 45 (bottom)
Terri Willis: 35 (left)
World Bank Photo Library: 19, 34, 82

ABOUT THE AUTHOR

Janet Pack is a writer who is intrigued by modern technology and scientific research. She is the author of *Lost Childhood*, true stories of children in World War II, written with Margaret Weis, and *California*, a young people's history of that state. Also a composer and vocalist, Mrs. Pack has created music to accompany a number of fantasy/science fiction novels.